The Birth of the Family

An Empirical Inquiry

Other Books by Jerry M. Lewis

No Single Thread: Psychological Health in Family Systems, 1976 (with W. R. Beavers, J. T. Gossett, & V. A. Phillips)

To Be a Therapist: The Teaching and Learning, 1978

How's Your Family?, 1979

Psychiatry in General Medical Practice, 1979 (edited with G. Usdin)

The Family: Evaluation and Treatment, 1980 (edited with C. K. Hofling)

Treatment Planning in Psychiatry, 1982 (edited with G. Usdin)

To Find a Way: The Outcome of Hospital Treatment of Disturbed Adolescents, 1983 (with J. T. Gossett & F. D. Barnhart)

The Long Struggle: Well-functioning, Working-class Black Families, 1983 (with J. G. Looney)

The Birth of the Family

An Empirical Inquiry

By

Jerry M. Lewis, M.D.

Senior Research Psychiatrist
Timberlawn Psychiatric Hospital
Timberlawn Psychiatric Research Foundation

Routledge
Taylor & Francis Group

LONDON AND NEW YORK

First published 1989 by Brunner/Mazel, Inc.

2 Park Square, Milton Park, Abingdon, Oxfordshire OX14 4RN
52 Vanderbilt Avenue, New York, NY 10017

Routledge is an imprint of the Taylor & Francis Group, an informa business

First issued in paperback 2019

Library of Congress Cataloging-in-Publication Data

Lewis, Jerry M.
    The birth of the family : an empirical inquiry / by Jerry M.
Lewis.
            p.   cm.
    Bibliography: p.
    Includes index.
    ISBN 0-87630-550-8
    1. Family—Texas—Dallas Metropolitan Area—Psychological aspects—
Longitudinal studies.   2. Parents—Texas—Dallas Metropolitan Area—
Psychology—Longitudinal studies.   I. Title.
    [DNLM: 1. Family.   2. Longitudinal Studies.   3. Marriage.
4. Parent-Child Relations.   5. Parents—psychology.   HQ 728 L674b]
HQ536.15.D2L48   1989
306.85—dc20
DNLM/DLC
for Library of Congress   89-9991
                                                                       CIP

ISBN 13: 978-0-87630-550-8 (hbk)
ISBN 13: 978-1-138-86909-7 (pbk)

Printed in the United Kingdom
by Henry Ling Limited

To our children
Jerry III, Cynthia, Nancy, and Tom,
with and for love.

Acknowledgments

Despite the importance of the family for individuals and society, funding the type of research reported in this volume is difficult. Funding for longitudinal research of any type is, perhaps, the most difficult to find. Thus, those individuals and agencies who have supported this longitudinal study of the development of well-functioning families are due a very special kind of gratitude.

At the top of the list of supporters are the Trustees of the Board of Timberlawn Psychiatric Research Foundation. During the six years of this project the Board has been led by David L. Florence and Alan D. Feld, and their leadership has been crucial to our success. The Board of Trustees has established a number of separate funds within the structure of the Foundation's Endowment Fund, and the yield from them has underwritten much of the research reported in this volume. The funds include:

The Charles and Sarah Seay Fund
The Crystal Charity Ball Fund
The Neiman-Marcus Fortnight Fund
The Samuel Roberts Noble Foundation Fund
The Kathy Gekiere Research Fund

and most recently through a generous bequest of the late Mrs. Cecil H. Green:

The Ida B. and Cecil H. Green Fund

In addition to these special endowment funds, the Foundation has received direct research grants that have supported our family research. Prominent among these have been grants from:

Mr. and Mrs. James R. Bower, Jr.
The Florence Foundation
The Hassie Hunt Foundation
The Highland Park Methodist Church
The Meadows Foundation
Mr. and Mrs. James Stewart
Mr. and Mrs. Fred J. Schoellkopf
The Barbara Kilby Estate
The Hogg Foundation for Mental Health
The Trull Foundation

The Friends of the Timberlawn Psychiatric Research Foundation, comprised of prominent women in the community, have each year sponsored a benefit that supplied the research staff with much-needed research funds. We are grateful to them for this support and their enthusiastic endorsement of the Foundation's work.

The Foundation has also received crucial support from Timberlawn Psychiatric Hospital, and during the years of the project reported in this volume the hospital has been led by Doyle I. Carson, M.D., Keith H. Johansen, M. D., Bryon L. Howard, M. D., and Mark J. Blotcky, M. D. We wish to express our gratitude to these clinical leaders and to all other members of the hospital staff.

Although the authorship of this volume is that of the writer, all research — and, in particular, longitudinal research — is the combined effort of many individuals. The family research at the Foundation began in the 1960s, and through the more than 20 years of effort, Virginia Austin Phillips, John T. Gossett, Ph. D., and the writer have worked together in a harmonious and, hopefully, productive ambiance. F. David Barnhart, M. A. joined us in 1972 and has played an important role since that time. The work reported herein is the current culmination of that collaboration, and I trust that Virginia, David, and John feel my gratitude.

The work reported in this volume brought to the Foundation two outstanding developmental psychologists who have served as Project Directors. Martha J. Cox, Ph. D. breathed life into the project and directed it for five years, to be replaced by Margaret Tresch Owen, Ph. D. who has provided leadership since 1984. These two remarkable scientists share authorship of Chapters 9 and 10, but in truth their efforts, encouragement, and critique are found on every page. V. Kay Henderson, M.S. has served as Assistant Project Director for the past several years, and she has been the glue that keeps this longitudinal project together.

In addition, a large number of colleagues have been involved in selected aspects of these reports. These colleagues include: Ted Asay, Ph. D., Barbara Berendzen, B. S., Martha Davison, M. D., Alexandria Doyle, Ph. D., Robert R. Hughes, B. S., Margaret Kaufmann, M. D., Jackie Kleumper, A.C.S.W., Pat P. Lewis, R. N., Nancy Margand, Ph. D., Annalisa Martin, Ph. D., Cynthia Lewis-Riedel, Ph. D., Lynda Scalf-McIver, B. A., Ana Suster, B. A., Stephen M. Tankersley, M. D., and Kathy Zilbermann, Ph. D.

Finally, my professional life is made possible by the excellence of my Administrative Assistant, Nannette Bruchey, who keeps the schedules, sends and pays the bills, and does all that makes a busy office run smoothly, in addition to typing my manuscripts. I hope that Nan knows my gratitude.

Contents

Part IV: Appendices

The Birth of the Family

An Empirical Inquiry

PART I

The Theoretical Context

CHAPTER 1

The Development of
Family Competence

This book presents findings from the initial stage of a longitudinal study of family development. At the broadest level it is the study of the development of family competence; it attempts to clarify the factors crucial for the growth of families that facilitate psychological health in their members. At a second level the study examines several constructs that are central to current models of the family life cycle. By studying young couples before and after the birth of their first child, it is possible to examine the assumption that change in family interactional structure is the normative transitional process for all families.

In the same manner the study allows empirical exploration of the construct of epigenesis as it applies to the family life cycle. Does, for example, the way in which couples resolve the issues involved in the stage of relationship formation predict how successfully their child will be incorporated into the family? The study also explores the impact of family of origin variables on psychological health, marital quality, and the transition to parenthood.

At a third, and more circumscribed level, the study illuminates a specified stage of family development, the transition to parenthood. The findings regarding changes in the marital relationship during the transition to parenthood add to and amplify a small group of studies by other investigators. By focusing also on the incorporation of the child into the family, a little explored but central feature of the transition, the study adds a crucial dimension to the understanding of the transition to parenthood.

In order to understand the development of this study, it is necessary to review briefly our earlier work and the central findings that evolved from it. In the mid 60s we began our family research as one part of a study of the outcome of hospital treatment for disturbed adolescents (Lewis, Gossett, & Phillips, 1971; Gossett, Meeks, Barnhart, & Phillips, 1976; Gossett, Barnhart, Lewis, & Phillips, 1977; Gossett, Lewis, & Barnhart, 1983). Impressed with the clinical observation that family variables appear sometimes to play a decisive role, we became interested in ways of systematically measuring family relationship variables.

As we studied the videotapes of families containing a hospitalized adolescent, it became clear that a control group of families with well-functioning adolescents was necessary. Such a group was studied, and within that group was a subgroup of warm, spontaneous, and clear families who attracted our attention. Thus began our interest in and study of psychologically healthy or highly competent families (Lewis, Beavers, Gossett, & Phillips, 1976).

Following the publication of the data from our initial study, we were frequently asked whether the findings were relevant for families at other socioeconomic levels. These questions led to a second study focusing on highly competent, lower income black families (Lewis & Looney, 1983). When we discovered that such families were, contrary to our hypotheses, much more alike than different from our initial sample of more affluent white families, it was decided to forego the study of other ethnic and socioeconomic samples and to begin longitudinal studies of family development. This decision was based on our realization that further descriptive studies of highly competent families, however important, would not inform as to how high levels of family competence come to be. Thus, the current study was designed and implemented.

As will be described in detail in a subsequent chapter, the initial task of this project was the systematic assessment of the structure of each couple's marital relationship during the prenatal period. Since our approach to that assessment was based on the methods and findings from our earlier two studies of families containing adolescent children, it is important to summarize what we observed in those studies. In this way I wish to introduce the broadest goal of the current study, studying the development of family competence over the family life cycle.

FAMILY COMPETENCE AND THE CONTINUUM OF FAMILY COMPETENCE

The central theoretical construct that guided our earlier research was that of family competence. We defined family competence as the extent to which a family accomplishes two cardinal tasks: producing psychologically healthy children who can function autonomously and enter into enduring relationships outside the family, and stabilizing the parents' personalities while facilitating their continuing development. These two tasks are important throughout the entire life cycle of the family and, as such, can be considered the basic perspective from which phase-specific family developmental tasks can be viewed.

The selection of these two tasks as measures of family competence reflects an inner-directed view — that is, we have focused on what the family "should" do for its members. Families "ought" to provide an interpersonal structure that facilitates the achievement of psychological health for the persons in the family. Although we believed this perspective to be important, it is not the only position possible. Reiss (1981), for example, focuses on the ways the family as a unit perceives and responds to the world about it. In some ways, Reiss's orientation is an "outer" perspective that complements our own.

The construct of family competence was thus developed in the context of understanding how families accomplish these two cardinal tasks. In earlier publications, we presented data supporting the idea that it is possible to construct a *Continuum of Family Competence* ranging from families who accomplish well these two tasks to families who fail to accomplish either task (Lewis et al., 1976; Lewis & Looney, 1983). We presented evidence that families on a particular point of the *Continuum of Family Competence* share many structural features, and that as one moves along the *Continuum* from most to least competent the structures of families change from flexible to rigid to chaotic. It seems clear, therefore, that the *Continuum of Family Competence* and the descriptions of the structural types of families at various points on the *Continuum* offer a possible beginning for a typology of families. This typology is based on systematically collected family data and, in our experience, has clinical relevance.

That it is possible to arrive at a global assessment of a family's competence is not, however, universally accepted. A number of family therapists and researchers eschew the construct of family competence, preferring to emphasize that each family has particular strengths and weaknesses. It may be that the idea of family competence is not acceptable to some because it seems to imply an elitist orientation. To deny, however, that some people and some social systems function better than others is to deny the validity of the structure of many systems of ordering behavioral data, including, for example, many approaches to understanding individual psychological functioning. In our approach to family competence, some families are assessed as functioning at optimal levels, others at levels of minimal to moderate dysfunction, and yet others at severely dysfunctional levels.

It is important, however, to emphasize that the criteria on which levels of competence are based are value judgments that are influenced decisively by the context in which the family is found. The criteria for evaluating family competence—that is, the extent to which a family produces children with certain capacities and facilitates continued personality development of the parents—are considered appropriate for families living in a context in which actual survival is reasonably assured. In a different context—one in which physical survival is a daily concern, for example—survival itself would be the primary criterion for assessing family competence. Very different patterns of organization, distribution of power, styles of communication, and ways of expressing and responding to affect might be expected to be associated with high levels of family competence in that context.

Ethnic and cultural factors also influence the criteria on which competence is assessed and, consequently, the types of family structure that will be associated with optimal functioning. For example, in cultures that emphasize male dominance, rigid patterns of authority and submission, formal rather than spontaneous communication, and past rather than future time, different criteria of family competence would be necessary. The issue of which criteria to use is crucial in studying various ethnic groups within the mainstream culture. McDermott and his associates, for example, are exploring family competence in four different ethnic groups in Hawaii (McDermott, Robillard, Char, Hsu, Tseng, & Ashton, 1983). A critical issue is whether after several generations of life within the mainstream culture it is more appropriate to assess Japanese-American families (for example) on the basis of the values and family patterns of Japan or those of mainstream, middle-class America.

Two issues become clear: values and the construct of competence are inseparable, and their relationship is complex. This is true for both individual and family competence. The central issue faced by researchers interested in what works best at the individual or family level is to be as explicit as possible about the values that underlie the assessment of competence and to underscore the ways in which different contexts influence what is possible.

The data from our earlier descriptive studies of families containing adolescent children support the existence of five basic types of families that can be located on the *Continuum of Family Competence*. In order of diminishing competence, they are the highly competent, the competent but pained, the dominant-submissive, the conflicted, and the severely dysfunctional. Although these are global descriptions of various family structures and several of the types have subtypes, they have, in our experience, relevance for clinical work with families.

The highly competent family is characterized by a parental relationship in which power is shared and there are high levels of closeness and commitment. Psychological intimacy is possible in such relationships. Despite the closeness, commitment, and intimacy, each parent is a well-individuated person capable of autonomous functioning. There is a clear boundary between the parental coalition and the children. The parenting style is neither permissive nor authoritarian; rather, it is authoritative. The parents listen to their children and often take their children's wishes, feelings, and opinions into consideration. The parents are, however, clearly in charge; there is no ambiguity about the distribution of power in the family.

Communication is open and spontaneous, a wide variety of feelings are expressed, empathy is often present, and there is a high probability of successful problem-solving. Family members are encouraged to be clear about opinions and feelings, and differences are tolerated or encouraged. Conflicts arise but are usually short-lived. Change is accommodated, losses are mourned openly. Overall, there is a warm, caring family mood. Humor is valued.

Highly competent families have evolved a basic family structure that encourages both attachment and separateness. Although severe and chronic stress can overwhelm such family systems, they are unusually resilient.

The competent but pained families are understood as being intermediate between highly competent and clearly dysfunctional families. They are competent from the perspective that their adolescent children have a high probability of psychological health. They are pained in that there is an underlying parental conflict around the issues of closeness and intimacy. The parental conflict has been contained in their relationship; it has not involved the children, at least in the sense of crossgenerational coalitions.

The marital pattern is most often that of the pursuer-pursued. When given the opportunity, one spouse (more frequently the wife) complains about the mate's emotional remoteness. Our investigations suggest that such mates are usually remote, intimacy-avoiding persons — that is, the complaining spouse is accurate in his or her description of the other. The more remote or pursued spouse, however, describes the complaining spouse as bitter, sour, chronically dissatisfied, and difficult to be close to, also an appraisal of some validity. Although each perceives the other with considerable accuracy, neither seems aware of his or her own contributions to the chronic impasse.

A second and less frequent pattern is the alternation of the roles of pursuer and pursued. Most often such cycles are of months or several years duration.

Thus, such marital relationships are characterized by little closeness, and often that which is present is related to shared interests in the activities of the children. Commitment is low, as each spouse may have relationships with others that involve greater sharing. Intimacy is absent. The distribution of power in the relationship is variable, but most often the pursued spouse has the upper hand in that he or she appears to control the level of closeness and intimacy in the relationship. Often each spouse is clearly individuated and capable of autonomous activity.

As a consequence of this type of parental relationship the family system is stilted, avoids open expression of affects, and does not have the clear warmth and affection of highly competent families. The children, however, have high probabilities of receiving independent ratings of high levels of individual psychological health, although, as a group, they are less spontaneous and open than children from highly competent families.

Competent but pained families can be understood as facilitating individuation and autonomy in family members, but do not encourage the development of strong attachments. Nevertheless, there is often a poignant investment in being a family, even if the major behavioral manifestation of that investment is a coming together around the activities and accomplishments of the children.

The template for the dominant-submissive family is a parental marriage that can be either complementary or conflicted. The complementary subtype involves a skewing of power that is satisfactory to both spouses much or most of the time. Although most often involving a dominant male and submissive female, the reverse is not uncommon. Conflicted dominant-submissive relationships in which the conflict is open and intense share properties with the conflicted marital structures to be discussed below. At lesser levels of conflict, the submissive spouse demonstrates a host of passive-aggressive mechanisms and crossgenerational alliances with one or more children that clearly have a quality of oppositionalism to the dominant spouse.

Dominant-submissive marriages are thus characterized by variable levels of closeness, the absence of intimacy, often high levels of commitment and frequently compromised individual autonomy, in addition to the skewed power.

Dominant-submissive families are rigid systems controlled (either subtly or openly) by the dominant parent. His or her beliefs, opinions, and feelings hold sway within the family, and negotiation is absent. Affect is not openly expressed, particularly warm, caring feelings. Task performance depends disproportionately on the skills of the dominant parent. The submissive spouse and children play but small roles and, as a consequence, often have problems developing fully autonomous self-systems.

Dominant-submissive family structures are dysfunctional in that there is an increased probability of the development of psychiatric syndromes in either the submissive spouse or the children. When such rigid systems are complementary, there is little likelihood that marital or family therapy will be sought. Rather, it is the development of a psychiatric syndrome in a family member that brings the marital couple or family to clinical attention.

Central to conflicted families is a chronically conflicted parental relationship. The conflict may present around a variety of issues (money, sex, discipline, etc.), but fundamentally the spouses are conflicted about the basic structure of their relationship. Each spouse attempts to be in the more powerful position, neither is willing to be submissive, and a more-or-less equal sharing of power does not seem possible. From a different perspective, the chronic conflict over the relationship structure can be understood as a system mechanism that facilitates contact without closeness or intimacy.

There are two prominent subtypes of conflicted marital relationships. The less severe subtype is conflicted intermittently. There are periods of weeks or months in which a growing sense of closeness evolves, only to be interrupted by the precipitation of a distance-producing conflicted phase that can also last weeks or months. The second subtype involves constant conflict without significant interruptions.

The conflicted marriage is thus characterized by little closeness, no intimacy, low levels of commitment, and a never-ending battle for power.

This type of parental relationship sets the interactional tone for the family system. Strife, arguments and, sometimes, physical assaults are commonplace. The children are drawn into the parental conflict in either stable or transient cross-generational alliances or distance themselves from the family if possible. Communication is inefficient, problem-solving is of poor quality, and manipulations, power plays, and deceitful maneuvers are common. There is little open expression of positive affects, often because they involve the threat of vulnerability. These are very dysfunctional and rigidly encoded systems and, although something of autonomous functioning can be learned in them, they do not facilitate the development of closeness in family members.

Severely dysfunctional families are of several types which are not often seen in research volunteer samples. One type is characterized by a symbiotic parental relationship. The spouses have fused their identities and are involved in massive mutual projection-introjection mechanisms. Often both spouses are individuals with poor levels of individuation, and their joint search for never-ending sameness may result in significant distortions of reality. To the observer, such systems seem chaotic, incomprehensible, and impervious to outside input. The children born to couples with symbiotic relationships can be incorporated into the symbiotic marital system or excluded from it with a resulting pervasive lack of attachment.

A second type of severely dysfunctional family is that in which one parent dominates the family with his or her psychotic distortions. Most often paranoid in nature, the dominant spouse's distortions are accepted by the more submissive spouse as an accurate reading of reality. This results in a marital system enmeshed by the acceptance of a paranoid stance about the world. Once again the children may or may not be caught up in the enmeshed parental relationship.

A third type of severely dysfunctional family is characterized by a parental relationship of almost complete alienation. In this type of family there is a pervasive unrelatedness, although each parent may have a primary alliance with a child. The overall family ambiance, however, is one of great distance and isolation rather than displaying the intense connectedness of the other two types.

These three types of severely dysfunctional families have been identified as family structures sometimes associated with the presence of a schizophrenic disorder in one or more family members. Family members either cling together in such an amorphous way as to obliterate individual boundaries or are so distant and isolated from each other that little if any closeness is experienced. Either way the family system is apt to be sorely deficient in problem-solving abilities. Most often these are disorganized, chaotic systems that relate in a paranoid fashion to their environments. Communication within the family is often fragmented and mystifying, and foci of attention are difficult to ascertain. Affects are either absent, inappropriate, or intense and primitive. Clinicians often find such family systems relatively impermeable to therapeutic intervention.

These five family types on the *Continuum of Family Competence* can be understood as structures that are flexible at the highly competent end of the *Continuum* and move toward rigidity and, ultimately, disorganization and chaos. The *Continuum of Family Competence* can be understood, then, at the most global level as moving from flexible → rigid → chaotic. In an earlier paper I have suggested that under conditions of sufficient stress a family's structure can be understood to change from flexible → rigid → chaotic (Lewis, 1986). Improvement in family functioning involves reverse changes in family structure; that is, from chaotic → rigid → flexible.

The descriptions of the five basic family types on the *Continuum of Family Competence* are developed more completely in earlier publications (Lewis et al., 1976; Lewis & Looney, 1983). For purposes of this presentation, however, they are offered to emphasize the central role of the parents' marital relationship structure as the crucial and basic template for the structure of the total family system.

MARITAL STRUCTURES

When one is interested in understanding the development of highly competent families, a useful place to start is with the parents' relationship prior to the birth of children. This we have done by studying our current sample of couples initially during the period prior to the birth of their first child. Such a starting point is a compromise, for the couples have been married variable periods of time, the first pregnancy comes after different lengths of marriage for different couples, and the impact of pregnancy itself on different types of marriages is an uncontrolled variable.

We made another assumption regarding the sample of couples, and that is that each couple's relationship structure is more or less in place; that during the courtship period and early marriage the couple has negotiated the basic parameters of their relationship: closeness, commitment, intimacy, autonomy, and power. Berman and Lief (1975) select similar dimensions as crucial determinants of marital dynamics.

Closeness is measured by the extent to which the spouses share interests, activities, friends, basic values, and pleasure in their sexual activities. Commitment is understood as the degree to which the marital relationship is experienced by both spouses as their primary affective relationship. Intimacy, in the sense used here, is the reciprocal sharing of vulnerabilities. Autonomy denotes the degree to which the relationship structure encourages individuality, differences, and independent functioning. Power is defined as overt interpersonal influence.

These five variables are postulated because they must be dealt with in the process of evolving a relationship with a hoped-for, long-term future. The negotiation of these issues is rarely overt; rather they are the metacontent of much that transacts during the stage of relationship formation. The results of the negotiation provide the basic structure of the relationship and establish the baseline balance of attachment and separateness within the relationship.

Currently, there is much emphasis on the ways in which one's family of origin influences and shapes the processes of mate selection and relationship formation. In a separate paper I have reviewed three theoretical approaches to the ways in which family of origin processes may influence early relationship formation (Lewis, 1988). These theoretical approaches are Meissner's (1978) transference model of marital dynamics, Reiss's (1981) model of underlying family paradigms, and Kantor and Lehr's (1975) model focusing on the transmission of key family roles from family of origin to marital relationship. Thus, it is my premise that family of origin factors play a role in the early, covert negotiation of closeness, commitment, intimacy, autonomy, and power that, in concert, result in the basic marital structure.

Two other research issues needed to be decided in planning this longitudinal research project. The first involved measurement and the second concerned the system of classification. Measurement raises the controversy regarding global measures of marital quality. Many who object to such measures say that all marriages have strengths and weaknesses and little is to be gained by making global judgments. My belief is that global measures of marital quality are supported both by public opinion and scientific study, and can be validated scientifically, such as by testing their predictive capacity. Measurement also raises a question about whether to rely on the spouses' ratings of marital satisfaction or on the systematic observations of marital behavior by presumed experts. This "insider-outsider" dilemma is common in social science research, and we have resolved it by using multiple sources of data (both insider and outsider) about marital quality to give a measurable level of marital competence.

A second research issue involves the need to order or classify the marital data. We have chosen to use the types of parental marital structures observed in the families containing adolescent children and to order those types along a *Continuum of Marital Competence.* Thus, in order of diminishing competence, we will classify the marital structures of the young couples in the current sample as highly competent, competent but pained, dominant-submissive (complementary), conflicted, and severely dysfunctional. The inference involved in this decision is that a continuum of relationship structures demonstrated to be valid at one stage of family life (adolescent children) will prove useful at a much earlier stage of family life. That, of course, is an empirical question and the data will inform us as to the wisdom of that decision.

THE FINDINGS OF OTHER INVESTIGATORS

Another source of information about the validity of the basic marital structures noted in our earlier research and used as a marital classification system in the current study is the extent to which identical or similar structures can be found in the data of other researchers using very different methods of investigation.

1. The Highly Competent Marriage

This type of marital relationship system is characterized by high levels of commitment, high levels of closeness, often with associated intimacy, and a relatively equal sharing of power. As individuals, the spouses have high levels of autonomy and, at the same time, are most often very relationship-oriented both within the marriage and within their families of origin, friendship groups, and occupational networks.

The study of this type of relational system in the parents of families containing healthy adolescent children prompted our interest in how such relationships evolve over time. The literature regarding such marital systems is relatively sparse, and much more can be found about dysfunctional marriages. One exception is the work of Cuber and Harroff (1965) who interviewed financially successful individuals whose marriages had lasted 10 years or more.

Cuber and Harroff's typology of marriage includes the Passive-Congenial, the Devitalized, the Conflicted-Habituated, the Vital, and the Total. Both the Vital and some of the Total marriages appear to share a number of characteristics with marital systems we would rate as highly competent, but Cuber and Harroff state that their marital types are not degrees of adjustment but "different kinds of adjustment." Vital marriages are characterized by an intense attachment which provides the "life essence" for both spouses. Central satisfactions are found through each other, but separate identities are maintained. The Total marriage is much like the Vital marriage, but the "points of vital meshing" are even more numerous. Of particular importance, however, is the authors' statement that they found that in some Total marriages the level of sharing was so intense that it was as if "neither spouse has, or has had, a truly private existence" (p. 60).

From my perspective, it seems that Cuber and Harroff have defined two very different types of marriages — one of which involves intense connectedness and the capacity for separateness and autonomy (the Vital and some of the Total marriages) and another type involving intense connectedness without separateness and autonomy (some of the Total marriages). I would predict very different life cycles for these two types of marriages. The type in which separateness and autonomy (Cuber and Harroff's "truly private existence") are absent will not, as a group, do as well in facilitating the health of the spouses over the years nor in raising healthy children as will those with an intense connectedness but the maintenance of separateness and autonomy.

Goodrich (1985) made a similar prediction about this cohort of the Cuber and Harroff sample. In his pioneering work with Raush, Ryder, and others, Goodrich (1968) proposes a beginning taxonomy of marriage based on their study of 50 couples, each of whom had been married for 3 months. A variety of interviews, questionnaires, observations, and experimental procedures were employed which resulted in diverse data which were then subjected to factor analysis.

This procedure resulted in the identification of eight patterns of marriage representing the positive and negative poles of four factors: 1) closeness or distance from the husband's family, 2) marital role orientation, 3) open conflict or harmony in marriage, and 4) closeness or distance from the wife's family. By examining closely the variables that load for each of these factors, it is possible to draw parallels between their study and our own typology, as well as similar parallels with the Cuber and Harroff typology. Several of Goodrich's factor analytically derived types appear to share the intense connectedness and the high levels of autonomy found in the marriages we describe as highly competent.

Kantor and Lehr's (1975) open family system also resembles our highly competent type of marital relationships. Kantor and Lehr describe the open system as structured around the core purpose of adaptation through consent. Throughout their description, the processes emphasized are negotiation, consensus, affective openness, high levels of responsiveness, tolerance for change, and, at the broadest level, the facilitation of high levels of both separateness and connectedness. These system qualities are characteristic of marital systems we describe as highly competent. In a similar way, Karpel's (1976) relational mode of dialogue with its balance of individuation and connectedness appears to parallel our description of highly competent relationships.

Families described by Reiss (1981) as "environment-sensitive" also share characteristics with highly competent marital systems. He describes these families as free of serious psychopathology, cooperative in problem solving, emphasizing mastery, and open to new experience. Such systems tolerate differences between family members, communicate openly, and are data-oriented. Reiss focuses on the family's transactions with the environment, deriving characteristics that are similar to some of the characteristics of our highly competent marriages.

Despite different methodologies, similarities exist between our empirically derived description of the highly competent marital system and the descriptions of certain types of relationships articulated by Cuber and Harroff, Goodrich and his colleagues, Kantor and Lehr, Karpel, and Reiss.

2. The Competent But Pained Marriage

These marital systems are characterized by moderate or low levels of commitment. One or both spouses may have a parent or friend with whom they have a closer alliance and to whom he or she may complain about the spouse. Each may share with investigators or therapists fantasies about extramarital affairs or their occurrence, or fantasies about divorce "after the children are grown." Closeness is a problem to both, and everyday, common-place exchanges replace intimacy. Individual autonomy is usually well developed. Both spouses have considerable power, but it usually is in very clearly defined areas which frequently follow traditional gender role assignments. Although the children and their activities play an obvious and important role in the spouses' commitment to the family as a whole, the fact that the children seldom are brought into the marital conflict in cross-generational alliances is a strength. The parents are able to contain the discord within their relationship and thus avoid apparent interference in the psychological development of the children.

In all likelihood, these competent but pained marital relationships are fairly common. Individual psychotherapists hear about them; marital therapists see and work with them. This type of relationship includes that which for many years has been called the "hysteric-compulsive" match. Beavers (1977) describes

both the individual and interactional characteristics of this type of relationship in which both spouses participate in the maintenance of significant
distance. Martin (1976) calls such relationships "the 'love-sick' wife and the
'cold-sick' husband" and suggests that the wife is incompletely individuated
and the husband is afraid of intimacy. Karpel (1976) sees this type of
relationship as derived from the relational mode of ambivalent fusion in
which both spouses are caught in the conflict between individuation and
fusion, but support an interactional pattern of "one partner distancing" in
which the roles of distancer and pursuer are relatively stable. Bowen's (1965)
description of "emotional divorce" which he related to the fear of fusion
suggests a strong descriptive parallel to the competent-but-pained relationship.
Several of Goodrich's (1968) factor analytically derived types are also similar,
as are components of the Cuber and Harroff (1965) "passive-congenial" and
"devitalized" marriages.

3. The Dominant-Submissive Marriage

Dominant-submissive marriages demonstrate various levels of commitment.
If the relationship is complementary, commitment can be very high; if the
relationship is significantly conflicted, commitment may be high or low.
Closeness is either at a moderate or at a low level, and intimacy is avoided.
Individuals usually have clear ego boundaries, but the submissive spouse may
not function autonomously because of his or her dependency. In these relational systems, each partner fears closeness and maintains considerable
distance. The dominant spouse both takes and is given the executive role in
distance-regulating processes.

Dominant-submissive marriages are common in clinical practice. Several of
the eight types of marriages in the typology of Goodrich (1968) also are
similar to subtypes of dominant-submissive marriages described above. He
describes "rational-controlled" defenses, lack of spontaneity and expressiveness,
husbands with primary occupational and economic orientations, and other
interactional characteristics common to dominant-submissive relationships.
There are also parallels between Kantor and Lehr's (1975) closed system and
complementary dominant-submissive marriages. Similarities include the presence of clearly designated authority, a major reliance on prescription, suppres-
sion of individual needs to the prescribed family code, clear mandates on each
family member's behavior, heavy emphasis on discipline, strong prohibitions
against overt requests for affection, nurturance, or closeness, and the possibility of rebellion and serious schism under circumstances of crisis.

Hafner (1986) has recently reviewed much of the literature involving marriage and psychosis, anxiety disorders, and affective disorders and finds

support for his sex-role perspective. He suggests that male-dominant marital structures play a role in the pathogenesis of a wide variety of psychiatric syndromes.

4. The Conflicted Marriage

In these marital systems power is bitterly contested, commitment is at a low level, closeness is minimal, and intimacy is totally lacking. Most often, both spouses are reasonably well-individuated persons capable of autonomous functioning.

Chronically conflicted marriages are common in clinical practice but relatively uncommon in research volunteer samples. There are excellent descriptions in the professional literature. Feldman (1979) has provided a rich description of the episodic type. Karpel's (1976) "continual conflict" relational type is similar to the chronically conflicted marriage, and Boszormenyi-Nagy (1965) emphasizes how chronic conflict may represent an uneasy balance between fusion and unrelatedness. Cuber and Harroff (1965) identify this marital type as the "conflict-habituated" marriage, and their description mirrors the one offered here.

Goodrich (1968) and his colleagues describe an openly conflicted marriage characterized by high levels of disagreement, shared unhappiness about the relationship, the absence of support from either spouse, strong individual identities with a weak identity as a couple, difficult decision-making, and the absence of empathy. All of these characteristics are similar to those we have found in the chronically conflicted marriage, and it seems clear that both Goodrich and our own group are describing the same type of marriage.

Lidz and his coworkers describe "marital schism" as the chronic failure of the spouses to achieve complementarity or role reciprocity (Lidz, Cornelison, Fleck, & Terry, 1957). Each spouse seeks to coerce the other, but is met by overt or covert defiance. Either spouse may be dominant — but conflict prevails. The partners undercut each other chronically, and neither finds satisfaction in the relationship. Mutual distrust is pervasive; husbands frequently occupy a depreciated position; wives are often rigid, cold, and distant. Either or both spouses may be fixed in dependent relationships with their own parents. The family is often split into two hostile factions.

The relationship of rigid marital systems of either the dominant-submissive or chronically conflicted type to Reiss's interpersonal distance-sensitive family type is not entirely clear, perhaps in part because Reiss's focus is so strongly on family problem-solving. He describes, however, a major theme of the individual's independence from the family, the individual's perception of the ideas of others as suggesting personal weakness, a pervasive isolation of family members from each other, reduced mastery, and a propensity of the family to produce family members with some form of serious character disturbance. These characteristics are similar to our findings in rigid, dysfunctional marital and family systems.

5. The Severely Dysfunctional Marriage

In severely dysfunctional marriages, commitment may vary from high to moderate, and a peculiar, sticky amorphousness may masquerade as closeness. The distribution of power within the relationship varies, and frequently there are close ties with families of origin (which themselves may be chaotic systems). As individuals, the spouses are often found to have low levels of psychological integration and defective capacities for autonomous functioning.

There are a number of graphic descriptions of marital relationships similar to that which we have called severely dysfunctional. Many of them spring from an interest in the contribution dysfunctional families make to the etiologies of the schizophrenias and have been presented by pioneers in family research. In particular, the writings of Bowen (1960), Wynne (Wynne & Singer, 1963), and Lidz and his collaborators (Lidz, Fleck, & Cornelison, 1965), have been instructive.

Although the specifics of their perspectives vary, each of these research groups focuses on the relational characteristics established by spouses with generally low levels of psychological integration and for whom there is either fusion or a schizoid unrelatedness. Underlying these two poles is a shared lack of individuation and a strong movement toward fusion, which is either operationalized or warded off with unrelatedness. The chaotic nature of their relationship results from cognitive distortions, mutual and interacting primitive projective systems, intense and shared fears of difference and change, shared irrational ideation, isolation from the surround, and instrumental ineffectiveness.

The description by Lidz and his colleagues of "marital skew," a relationship dominated by the serious psychopathology of the dominant spouse, is identical to that we have described as intermittently chaotic (Lidz et al., 1957).

Minuchin and his colleagues describe enmeshed families, one group of which shares characteristics with chaotic families (Minuchin, Baker, Rosman, Liebman, Milman, & Todd, 1975). They emphasize high levels of interdependency, intrusions on personal boundaries, and poorly differentiated individual self-perceptions. An individual's life space is impinged upon, and family members often speak for each other. Executive hierarchies are weak and confused. Change and growth are not facilitated, denial is rampant, and autonomy is a difficult accomplishment.

Sharpe (1981) describes the "symbiotic marriage," a pathologically extreme form of mutual dependency in which each partner relates to the other as an extension of self. She suggests that the prototype for this relationship is the mother-infant symbiosis in the first year of life, and with this emphasis builds a psychoanalytic object relationship model stressing the role of projective identification and the "trading of dissociated parental introjects." Sharpe describes three types of symbiotic couples: the sadomasochistic, the pseudo-mutual, and the bickering-blaming. These three types and our description of three types of severely dysfunctional marriages have much overlap.

Reiss's (1981) consensus-sensitive family system has many parallels to some forms of what we call chaotic marital and family systems. He describes the intense efforts of such families to maintain sameness and close agreement and to avoid discussion through hastily forged consensus, often attained through oversimplifying and distorting environmental cues. Because they solve problems by maintaining close agreement among family members, mastery of problems is reduced. The outside world is perceived as potentially dangerous to family ties. It seems clear that Reiss believes there are degrees or levels of consensus sensitivity; at the functional level he uses southern Italian families as an example, whereas at a lower level of functioning he notes that consensus-sensitive families are apt to be found to contain schizophrenic offspring. It is, then, the form of consensus-sensitive family that contains such disturbed children that is similar to that which we call chaotic marital or family systems.

Goodrich (1968) and his colleagues do not describe a chaotic marital type, perhaps because such couples seldom volunteer for marital and family research and presumably were absent from their sample. The same presumption may be valid for the Cuber and Harroff (1965) sample and, as a consequence, the varieties of chaotic marriages are not found in their typology. Kantor and Lehr's (1975) "flawed random" type of system has some parallels with this description of chaotic families — in fact, they use the descriptor "truly chaotic" for one subgroup. They describe members' experiencing "shifting images" and "jarred rhythms," inconstancy, turbulence, and a pervasive lack of discipline. Their description, however, lacks the emphasis placed here on merger, fusion, and symbiosis with resultant absence of autonomy.

Thus, it appears from this selective review of the work of other investigators that the five basic types of marital structures identified in our earlier work with families containing adolescent children have been described elsewhere as well. Other investigators, however, do not describe the relative adaptive capacity of the different types as we do by the construction of the *Continuum of Marital Competence*. Whether this ordering of the type of marital structures along such a continuum proves useful may be illuminated by the data from this study.

The description of these strategic decisions made during the planning stage of this project, along with the presentation of the five basic marital structures, provides the starting point for our study of the development of family competence. Some of the questions that may be answered by the data follow:

Can the five types of marital structures be identified in this sample of young couples?

Does this approach to classifying marital structures encompass the marriages of all the couples in this sample?

What role does the level of individual health of the spouses play in the quality of the marriage?

Do family of origin factors influence marital quality and/or the level of family functioning after the birth of the first child?

Are the responses of the various marital structures to parenthood predictable or not?

Which types of marital structures are most prone to crisis and structural reorganization during the transition to parenthood?

Does the type of prenatal marital structure influence the way in which the child is incorporated into the family?

These are but illustrative questions; there are many more that can be posed and answered by the data from this early stage of this longitudinal family research project. At a broader level, however, it is hoped that these data and those that will follow can provide insights into the pathway (or pathways) leading to high levels of family competence.

CHAPTER 2

Selected Theoretical Issues

This research project addresses three major areas. The first area, the development of family competence, was the major focus of Chapter 1. In this chapter the second major area will be addressed: the small number of key theoretical issues regarding current family life cycle theory that may be illuminated by the data of this project. These issues are 1) structural stability and change during a normative family life cycle transition, 2) epigenesis as it may apply to the family life cycle, and 3) the role of family of origin factors in a family life cycle transition. Before turning to these three theoretical issues, however, a brief description of my perception of the current status of the family life cycle perspective is indicated.

Throughout recorded history scholars have attempted to bring order to an understanding of the course of human life by dividing it into stages. This partitioning of life into segments facilitates the organization of data and is a step in dealing with the inordinate complexity involved in studying the human life course. It is easy, however, to be overly concrete by treating stages of the life cycle as real rather than as convenient abstractions. As pointed out by Gurman (1983), a problem associated with the life cycle conceptualization is the common nominalist fallacy that by naming a phenomenon one understands it.

Another perplexing problem is that in describing a particular stage of life it is necessary to focus on or emphasize certain processes at the expense of others. With a few exceptions, for example, current clinical theory is skewed heavily in the direction of separation-individuation phenomenology at the expense of a balancing relational focus. Finally, the intuitive appeal of the life cycle perspective is so strong that it is easy to overlook how few empirical studies support it. Indeed, Neugarten (1979), a distinguished investigator of adult development, cautions against regarding even such basic life cycle constructs as regularity and "dramatic transitions" as normative in lieu of available data.

The extension of the life cycle perspective from the individual to the family is hardly surprising because of the need to organize this large body of complex data. What may be somewhat surprising is the speed with which the family life cycle has become a central construct — perhaps even the dominant construct — in family therapy. Gurman (1983) emphasizes that the construct of progressive stages in the family life cycle is a part of all major theories of family functioning, and recognition of the construct is considered essential for effective family therapy.

Even at the level of theory only a modest start has been made. Hill and Mattessich (1979), for example, emphasize that current family development theories are entirely descriptive. No family theorist has dealt systematically with the key issues that have perplexed the entire field of life span development. Spanier and his colleagues present evidence to suggest that the family life cycle perspective may be the preferred approach to certain research questions, but other methods of stratification (age or length of marriage) are equally good — or better — perspectives for other research questions (Spanier, Sauer, & Larzelere, 1979).

Finally, remarkably few longitudinal studies of families utilize an interactional approach in which relationship processes are studied directly, and there are few systematically collected empirical data with which to test the growing body of speculations about the development of families over time. Support for these speculations comes primarily from the arena of family therapy. Even though family therapy may provide provocative ideas about family development, such data are suspect as support for specific theories. Families who are functioning effectively are seldom seen by therapists, and a distorted view of the developmental process may result because therapists tend to find what they look for in complex therapeutic interactions, and data from the clinical arena come disproportionately either from families under stress or from chronically dysfunctional families.

The distortion caused by such reliance on clinical samples surfaced, for example, several decades ago when the clinician's image of normal adolescence was influenced by a theoretical construct called "adolescent turmoil." Adolescents who experienced this stage of life with little or no obvious turmoil were suspect; dramatic crises, rebellion, and tumultuous relationships were seen as the norm. Only when systematic studies included nonclinical samples of adolescents did a more comprehensive understanding of adolescent development develop (Oldham, 1978). I believe a similar process has occurred in the literature of the family life cycle with the result being a model of the family life cycle significantly distorted by the absence of either research or clinical data about families who function effectively. Perhaps as a consequence, crisis and sudden major changes in structure are emphasized, and families that traverse developmental transitions without crisis and major structural change are apt to be seen as dysfunctional.

In sum, the broad and enthusiastic adoption of the family life cycle perspective in clinical arenas has not been tempered by an appreciation of the incompleteness of current theories and the inadequacies of available empirical data.

STABILITY AND CHANGE IN FAMILY STRUCTURE

At a general level, the family life cycle perspective proposes that relatively long periods of structural stability are punctuated by transitional periods in which a crisis precipitates change in family structure. Under ideal circumstances, the changed structure renders the family more proficient in dealing with the changes in their inner or outer world. Under less than ideal circumstances, the family is unable to respond to the altered context with appropriate structural change and becomes fixed at a level of structural organization inappropriate to the changed context. Such periods of fixed structure in the life of the family involve increased vulnerability to the development of symptomatic states by one or more family members. A third possibility, suggested by Barnhill and Longo (1978), is that family structure regresses to less competent levels during transitional periods. Such a possibility then provides three potential outcomes of a developmental transition — one of which is positive (crisis and constructive change) and two of which are negative (failure of the family structure to change and regression).

This description raises questions about family structure, developmental transitions, and structural change: What is family structure? If structure is defined as interactional patterns with a slow rate of change, the measurement of change in family structure may be reasonably complex. If, however, family structure is defined in terms of number of members, change is measured easily. Many students of the family life cycle emphasize that family structure changes — without their being explicit about their definition of structure. If structure is defined as recurring interactional patterns, and the couple's relationship pattern, for example, is dominant-submissive, the issue becomes whether the structure of the relationship remains the same following the birth of the child or alters, either in the direction of increasing egalitarianism and closeness or regresses to increasing conflict and distance. Using such a definition of structure leads to a set of hypotheses about whether structural change occurs (in some, most, or all families), the direction of change, the duration of change, and the adaptive value of the change.

There are three theoretical positions about the process of change in family structure. The first position is that there is remarkable stability to family structure within and/or across transitions. Representative of this position is the work of Raush and his colleagues (Raush, Barry, Hertel, & Swain, 1974). This work is unusual in that it involves the systematic collection of empirical data. The investigators focused their study on patterns of conflict resolution during the early stage of marriage. They reported that stable patterns are established early in the marriage (by four months) and are consistent over the following two or more years. In the cohort of their sample in which a child was born during this time, there was no evidence that the transition to parenthood was a crisis resulting in a basic change in the pattern of conflict resolution. The changes, although significant, were not major. They did not appear to be the changes of the magnitude usually described as "second order," "trans-formations," or "leaps." Indeed, the authors' overall conclusion emphasized the stability of patterns of conflict-resolution over time.

A second position about structural change during the family life cycle involves the concept of predictable change. My position (Lewis, 1986) involves the idea that change in structure is predictable (flexible $\rightleftharpoons$ rigid $\rightleftharpoons$ chaotic) in response to severe stress, and support is found in the work of Reiss (1981) and Anthony (1970). However, that focus was on severe stress and not on the stress of life cycle transitions. Berman and Lief (1975) propose, however, a model of normal marital development over time that emphasizes predictable change. Their theory, derived in part from the work of Levinson and colleagues (1978), proposes predictable changes in specific dimensions of the marital relationship (commitment, intimacy, power, and boundaries) over the life cycle.

Recently, Combrinck-Graham (1985) described a theoretical model, the Family Life Spiral, which also posits predictable changes in family structure. She suggests that all family systems move back and forth between periods with a stronger *centrifugal* focus — in which the emphasis is upon increased distance, separation-individuation, and autonomy — and periods of a stronger *centripetal* focus — in which there is "enmeshment, diffusion of interpersonal boundaries, and a high degree of resonance among individuals within the system" (p. 145). During centripetal periods there are clearer boundaries around the family system in its relationship with the context. As the family moves toward a centrifugal period (as when children enter school), the system must be able to open up and facilitate increased emotional distance between family members and increased involvement with the surround. In effect, the family must be able to dismantle the family structure and free family members to separate, individuate, and become autonomous. Each cycle of developmental growth within the family is comprised of four phases: centripetal → transitional → centrifugal → transitional, and then the cycle begins anew.

Combrinck-Graham's model also delineates the ways the original marital or family structure may influence the developmental sequence as, for example, a system with either too much connectedness (enmeshment) or too little connectedness (distance) may not be able to respond to developmental challenges with contextually appropriate increase in centrifugality or centripetality. Yet even in these instances, the resulting "developmental misfit" is predictable.

Wynne (1984) proposes a model that incorporates both predictable and unpredictable change. Wynne's interest in the epigenesis of relational systems starts from the premise that no one has specifically applied the epigenetic principle to relational systems. He suggests that four relational processes appear to unfold epigenetically to form the basis for understanding family development: Attachment and caregiving (affectional bonding), communicating (sharing foci of attention and exchanging meaning), joint problem solving (and renewable sharing of interests and activities), and mutuality (patterns of reengaging, renewing, and deepening the preceding modes of relatedness).

Each of these relational processes can have either a positive or a negative pole, the latter referring to some form of distancing, divergence, differentiation, or relational failure. Whether at the positive or negative pole, the specific processes are presumed to unfold in an orderly sequence and are, therefore, predictable. Wynne's model, however, allows for something other than a smooth, continuous, and predictable unfolding as new ingredients are randomly introduced or created, and the observer may perceive periods of discontinuous destabilization.

Currently, much of the family therapy literature emphasizes the third position, that the family responds to developmental transitions with unpredictable changes in the family structure. Carter and McGoldrick (1980), Terkelsen (1980), and Hoffman (1980), are representative. Carter and McGoldrick (1980) discuss discontinuous change as a leap that occurs when a family's usual homeostatic mechanisms do not suffice during a normative crisis. The crisis is characterized by confusion, inconsistencies, and paradoxical injunctions, all of which are considered necessary prerequisites for a creative transformation in family structure.

Terkelsen's (1980) model suggests that a new primary need appearing in one family member sets in motion a sequence of need attainment in the family, which involves a temporary period of destabilization out of which evolves a new family structure. Destabilization is characterized by conflict, frustration, and anxiety within the family. There are also associated processes in which the family gives up significant aspects of its old structure, and these losses are grieved. Resolution of the processes of structural change occurs through trial and error, but involves extensive revision of the family's consensual reality. Terkelsen describes these normative life cycle changes as transformations and proposes that the form of the resulting structural reorganization is not predictable.

Hoffman (1981) offers a rich and detailed account of the changes in family structure during normative transitions and credits much of her model to the work of Bateson (1978), Maruyana (1968), Prigogine (1969), and Dell (Dell & Goolishian, 1979). Inevitably, all families become unbalanced as the power relationships between the generations shift. She describes a series of steps starting with the failure of homeostatic, first-order mechanisms to deal with the altered developmental context. Increasing dissonance within the family leads to a crisis, and the "corrective sweeps" generated in an effort to deal with the crisis get out of control. This runaway situation results in a spontaneous leap to a new level of integration, a return to the previous homeostatic level, or disintegration of the family.

Hoffman stresses unpredictability, but softens this stance, stating that although the nature of the structural changes cannot be foreseen, probabilities can be assessed in some cases. She also questions whether there are levels of organization through which families must move when undergoing transformations. In this regard she describes homeostatic plateaus or ranges within which family functioning and structure can be maintained by first-order changes. It is but a small step to posit that different families have either broad or narrow homeostatic plateaus, moving us to a consideration of the influence of the existing family structure on the processes of change.

I suggest that the structural changes experienced by families during transitional periods are influenced in a significant way by the level of structural organization (or family competence) characteristic of the family during the preceding, stable period. As noted in an earlier publication, families with higher levels of competence have a greater variety of coping skills (homeostatic mechanisms) and more structural flexibility (Lewis, 1986). As a consequence, they are in a position either to maintain their structural integrity or to evolve new structures that are adaptive to a changing context.

Dysfunctional families have more limited coping skills, and the rigidity of their overall structural integration makes them less effective at adapting to changing circumstances. Such rigid family structures (dominant-submissive and conflicted) comprise the bulk of family therapists' work and are—by virtue of their structural rigidity—the ones likely to change suddenly and unpredictably. The change is unpredictable because it may be either to greater closeness and egalitarianism or to greater distance, conflict, and, ultimately, disorganization.

EPIGENESIS

The concept that relational systems such as marital or family systems pass through transitional periods in which certain developmental tasks must be faced is central to current thinking about the family life cycle. A closely related construct, family epigenesis, involves the idea that the developmental transitions at a particular stage of marital or family development are built upon the successful completion of earlier developmental transitions.

This construct—borrowed from the individual developmental theory of Erikson (1963)—is dealt with cautiously (if at all) by many current students of family development. Relatively few theoretical models attend the construct, or they do so with only brief and abstract references. I have been unable to find empirical data either to support or to refute the construct of epigenesis in the development of family systems. Indeed, despite the acceptance of the construct by students of individual development, there are also few empirical studies that test the epigenetic base of individual development. Vaillant's (1977) work is an exception.

Some factors that account for the lack of empirical data on family epigenesis were pointed out over 20 years ago by Magrabi and Marshall (1965). They emphasized the need both to identify with specificity the developmental challenges or tasks of each transitional period and to identify behaviors that indicate their accomplishment. They also present a "game tree" model of developmental tasks which predicts a variety of outcomes without specifying their adaptive significance. Magrabi and Marshall's call for the delineation of specific developmental challenges for families and descriptions of the behavior that indicates the accomplishment of these challenges has not been answered.

Developmental challenges continue to be defined globally and loosely (formation of a marital system, realignment of previous relationships, and encouraging individual autonomy, to name a few). Operational definitions of the failure or success of their accomplishment are not to be found.

At the level of family theory, Wynne's (1984) work is an exception. He offers a clear epigenetic framework and describes both successful and dysfunctional outcomes. By way of illustration, Wynne proposes that the initial task of a relationship is the development of attachment, defined primarily as mutual caretaking. When that is successfully accomplished, the likelihood of developing adequate communication patterns is augmented.

Three types of dysfunctional attachment are proposed: emotional overinvolvement, "flat" detachment, and criticism/withdrawal. These dysfunctional types of attachment can lead respectively to specific communication abnormalities: amorphous communication deviation, guarded communication, and fragmented communication. Four patterns of communication (functional, amorphous, guarded, and fragmented) are posited to lead to specific types of joint problem-solving. Wynne's theory clearly has a strong epigenetic component and is, therefore, an exception.

I suggest that the developmental challenge of early marriage is the establishment of a relational structure in which both spouses find a balance of separateness and connectedness that facilitates their psychological health and that of their children. Commitment, power, closeness, intimacy, and autonomy have been proposed as the key processes in negotiating this relational balance. These processes have been operationalized by developing rating scales to be used with both individual and interactional data. Thus, the criteria called for by Magrabi and Marshall (1965) in defining the developmental challenges of early relationship formation have been met. However, the indicators of the successful accomplishment of the developmental challenges of early relationship formation remain unsettled. Should success be defined as the establishment of the marital structure that proved to be highly competent (as in our studies of families containing adolescent children), or should success in accomplishing this early developmental challenge be defined as the establishment of any type of marital structure as long as it is associated with high levels of satisfaction expressed by both spouses? My position and hypotheses favor competence over satisfaction as a predictor of subsequent success with the transition to parenthood.

Our research design did not allow us to test directly the process of relationship formation in our sample. This is because the couples in this sample had been married for from less than one year to 15 years. We did not have the opportunity to study these couples as they were evolving their relationships. Their relationships are considered to be "in place" at the start of the study or, stated differently, the initial relationship structure (and its level of competence) had already been "negotiated" by the couple.

When the focus is turned to the developmental challenges of the next stage of family development, the transition to parenthood, the literature provides only rather global definitions. My position is that each set of new parents must make many accommodations, and the principal developmental challenges involve incorporating the child into the family and supporting the continuing development of the parents' relationship.

Since each couple was studied prenatally, the opportunity was present to predict the extent to which they met the developmental challenges of early parenthood. In this regard, I believe we have data relevant to the construct of family epigenesis in analyses regarding the impact of prenatal marital structures on the incorporation of the child into the family.

FAMILY OF ORIGIN

The third issue regarding family life cycle theory that our data may illuminate involves the role of family of origin influences on here-and-now family development. Family of origin data were collected through interviews, questionnaires, and marital discussion tasks, and are used to answer the very general questions, "Do family of origin factors appear to influence the couple's experiences during the transition to parenthood and, if so, in what ways?"

The role of family of origin influences on family development is given considerable weight by a large number of students of the family. Discussions of family of origin influences are prominent in the work of Bowen (1978). More recently, Combrinck-Graham (1985) has suggested that the interactions at three generational levels must be studied in order to understand that which is going on at any one level. Internalized family of origin influences are central to psychoanalytically derived theories of marital and family systems, and the theories of Meissner (1978) and Framo (1976) are illustrative.

To review all the theoretical literature is beyond the scope of this chapter, but it seems fair to suggest that family of origin influences occupy a central role in much of family theory, therapy, and training. It is, therefore, surprising that there is so little published systematic research. The majority of the research has been reported by developmental psychologists and was reviewed in an earlier publication (Cox, Owen, Lewis, Riedel, Scalf-McIver, & Suster, 1985). The research in general focuses on the relationship between mothers' recall of their experiences with their parents and various measures of parenting skills with their own children. For the most part, these studies report a positive relationship between favorable recall of the family of origin and both parenting sensitivity and secure attachment with their children.

Recently Belsky and Pensky (in press) have brought these data together in an illuminating review. With few exceptions, the published studies rely on retrospective accounts of family of origin factors, and demonstrate a variety of significant associations between positive recollections of family of origin and marital satisfaction and measures of effective parenting.

When the focus is turned to longitudinal studies, similar positive associations are found. Most of these studies report adolescent or early adulthood recollections of family of origin factors and subsequent midlife personality characteristics, quality of object relationships, or marital stability and satisfaction. Vaillant and his coworkers, for example, describe significant correlations between family of origin factors and the quality of midlife object relationships (close friendships, good family relationships, and stable marriages) and work success in samples first studied as college students and inner city youths (Vaillant, 1974; Vaillant & Milofsky, 1980). Brooks (1981) reports similar findings for both males and females in data from the Oakland and Berkeley growth studies. Thomas and Greenstreet (1973) report that young adult male medical students who describe lack of closeness to parents are more apt to subsequently develop mental illness, malignant tumors, and commit suicide.

Elder and his colleagues also report data from the Oakland and Berkeley growth studies (Elder, Caspi, & Downey, 1986). Their report is distinguished by the fact that three generations were studied directly, thus avoiding reliance on retrospective accounts of family of origin factors. Adult subjects who recalled their parents negatively were more likely to develop unstable personalities and conflicted marriages. Their children were found to have more than anticipated behavioral problems and, as adults, demonstrated personality instability, marital conflict, and ineffective parenting. In turn, their children were more apt to demonstrate dysfunctional behavioral controls, indicating a recycling process.

Taken as a whole, these studies add an empirical base to theoretical and clinical constructs. There are, however, several questions remaining. One is the issue of variables that may mediate the family of origin influences. Belsky and Pensky (in press) review data supporting the role of individual personality characteristics as the connection between family of origin influences and here-and-now relationships. Whether the here-and-now outcomes are marital satisfaction, parenting effectiveness, or depressive and lonely states, retrospective accounts of family of origin variables are significantly associated. Belsky and Pensky conclude that these data are consistent with the mediating role of personality variables, but note that behavioral genetic interpretations cannot be ruled out.

A second problem is that the statistical associations between family of origin variables and here-and-now relationships, although significant, account for but a modest amount of variance. It thus appears that although intergenerational continuity is supported by these studies, considerable intergenerational discontinuity remains to be understood. Belsky and Pensky point to the work of Rutter and his colleagues as suggesting that the discontinuities are lawful—that is, to a significant degree, predictable (Rutter, 1982; Rutter & Quinton, 1984). In studying girls who were raised in residential programs and, for the most part, had poor outcome reflected by personality disorders and dysfunctional marriages, the investigators explored the lives of the subgroup who turned out well. These girls had experienced school positively, had married a supportive spouse, and were later rated as effective mothers.

Although it is not known why this subsample of "good outcome" girls had positive school experiences and married well, the findings suggest the nature of the processes that can redirect developmental trajectories (i.e. positive experiences which are effectively remedial).

These relatively few empirical studies of family of origin influences are primarily concerned with individual outcomes. There is not a comparable body of empirical literature regarding marital and family outcomes. The design of our study will allow us to explore the impact of prenatally collected family of origin influences on marital quality before and after the birth of the first child and on the incorporation of the child into the family. Thus, we should be able to develop greater insight into the ways in which family of origin variables influence relationship structures and processes.

There are other theoretical issues involving family life cycle theory upon which our data may shed light. It was, however, the three constructs of structural change, epigenesis, and family of origin that played an important role in designing the study, and for that reason something of my perspective of their theoretical importance has been briefly summarized.

CHAPTER 3

The Transition to Parenthood: A Selective Review

The third general area that this research project addresses is the transition to parenthood. Two developmental challenges were selected with which to evaluate the outcome of this important transition: the stabilization or improvement in the parents' relationship and the successful incorporation of the child into the family. As far as can be ascertained, there have been no direct studies of the incorporation of the child into the family, and we hope our conceptual and methodologic contributions add to the understanding of the richness and complexity of this family transition.

There is, however, a relatively large literature exploring the relationship between the marital relationship and parenthood. Two seminal studies provided impetus for this literature: Simmel's (1902) turn of the century sociological conceptualization of the consequences of the change from dyad to triad and Hill's (1949) classical studies of families under stress.

In 1957, LeMasters published his study of the decline in marital satisfaction associated with the transition to parenthood, and this was followed by a number of other studies (Benedek, 1959; Dyer, 1963; Hobbs, 1965, 1968; Hobbs & Cole, 1976; Hobbs & Wimbish, 1977; Jacoby, 1969; Meyerowitz & Feldman, 1966; Rapoport, 1963; Russell, 1974). As Cox (1985) has recently emphasized, the interpretation of these studies (mostly showing declines in marital satisfaction across the transition) is confounded by conceptual and methodological problems, including the fact that families were studied after the birth of the child, retrospective self-reports of marital satisfaction prior to parenthood were used, the concept of crisis was often either not defined operationally or used in different ways by different researchers, and control groups of couples not experiencing parenthood were omitted.

As a consequence, the decline in marital satisfaction, particularly noted in wives, could not be clearly understood. Does it represent the direct consequences of parenthood and, if so, which aspects of parenthood? Does it represent a manifestation of partpartum "blues"—that is, is it a part of an increasingly negative orientation to life in general? Does it represent changes in marital satisfaction that occur with time in the absence of parenthood? Does it represent a leveling off of an earlier euphoria associated with pregnancy? These and other factors may all be involved. At another level, however, the changes reported are group means. What distinguishes those spouses and couples for whom there is little or no decline or even augmented marital satisfaction through the transition from those individuals and couples for whom there are moderate or severe declines?

Another development in the literature involves the gradual addition of measures beyond marital satisfaction in the attempt to understand the changes associated with parenthood. Although most of the new measures continue to be self-reports, a few studies have included outsiders' observations using a variety of rating or scoring systems.

Because this report concerns itself with changes in the marital relationship through the transition to parenthood, it appears most appropriate to examine in greater detail several studies that are most relevant to this concern. I have selected from a number of studies several that indicate that the quality of the marital relationship is one of the most important correlates of successful adaptation to parenthood.

The work of the Cowans and their collaborators is one of the richest sources of information. In a series of presentations and publications, these researchers have examined in detail a large number of important variables (Cowan, Cowan, Coie, & Coie, 1978; Cowan & Cowan, 1983; Cowan & Ball, 1981; Cowan & Cowan, 1981; Cowan & Cowan, 1985a; Cowan & Cowan, 1985b).

Cowan and Cowan present a coherent theoretical framework for their research. The most abstract premise is that the overriding task in the family is establishing a balance between individuality and coupleness, and in this regard our theoretical system (as well as those of others) is in agreement. In the attempt to get at the possible ways that couples and families organize and function, they emphasize interrelated dimensions: the psychological sense of self of each spouse, the social role behavior of each spouse, and the spouses' communication patterns. They state that there is no single ideal pattern of sense of self, social roles, and communication patterns that is more adaptive than others. The arrival of the baby will be accompanied by individual and couple disequilibrium, some of which is a necessary condition for developmental growth. As one part of this disequilibrium, couples tend to adopt traditionally defined and more differentiated roles during times of stressful transitions, including the birth of the first child.

In their initial study, the Cowans find support for "significant amounts of disequilibrium for each individual and couple" (Cowan et al., 1978, p. 320). Some aspects of this disequilibrium are experienced as stress, and at high levels dysfunction is produced. Other aspects of the disequilibrium provide the impetus for growth and a "more optimal balance between partners" (p. 321). Presumably, this refers to a more optimal balance of individuality and coupleness.

In a more recent report from the same study, the Cowans discuss several additional variables that they measured (Cowan, Cowan, Heming, Garrett, Coysh, Curtis-Bowles, & Boles, 1985). This results in five domains that they have studied: individual family members, marital interaction involving roles and communication, each parent-child relationship, intergenerational relationships, and the balance between life stress and social support. Their primary hypothesis has been that negative changes occur in each domain during the transition to parenthood.

The data from their study partially supported their hypothesis. They found that spouses becoming parents and a control group not becoming parents both report stable levels of individual self-esteem, life stress, and descriptions of families of origin. Of all measures of marital roles and communication, childless couples tended to remain stable or change positively, whereas couples becoming parents experienced negative change. Men in this latter group experienced less negative change than women, indicating a greater involvement in and impact from parenthood for mothers.

Marital satisfaction declined from pregnancy through 18 months postpartum, and the decline was most dramatic from pregnancy to six months postpartum for wives and from six to 18 months postpartum for husbands. Of particular importance to our perspective, however, is the Cowans' finding of consistency in the rankings of their individual and couple measurements over time. This confirms the empirical work of Belsky and emphasizes that individuals and couples doing relatively well or relatively poorly prior to parenthood are found to be doing relatively well or relatively poorly after parenthood (Belsky, Spainer, & Rovine, 1983).

From their findings, the Cowans suggest that the key intervening variable in understanding the decline in marital satisfaction following the birth of a baby was the increasing role differences between spouses that led to increased marital conflict and growing marital dissatisfaction. They argue that the differences between the spouses take the form of increasing gender differentiation — that is, both spouses appear to adopt more conventional gender roles after the birth of the child, and this appears to be the root of the increasing differences between them, differences that lead to increasing conflict, which increases marital dissatisfaction. They state: "Partners already vulnerable from lack of sleep and major shifts in their senses of themselves, their roles in the worlds of family and work, and their intimate relationships, find themselves startled by unexpected differences and increased conflict" (Cowan et al., 1985, p. 476).

Although evidence is presented suggesting that it is the role of gender role differentiation → conflict → marital dissatisfaction pathway that may be most informative, in another paper from this study Boles (1983) suggests that it is not the arrangement of roles (egalitarian versus traditional) that is operative, but the spouses' satisfaction with how the roles are arranged.

In another paper from the Cowans' study, Heming (1981) presents data about the early identification of couples at risk. Utilizing several approaches to rating levels of marital quality, she reports that couples at risk during the transition to parenthood involve new mothers who see their husbands as sharing less baby care, who describe marital decision-making as more unbalanced, and who are less satisfied with their more gender stereotypic role arrangements than are women from couples considered as low risk. For new fathers in the high-risk group, other data indicate diminished involvement in all aspects of baby care, increased marital conflict, and decreased marital satisfaction. In addition, from these and other data, Heming states: "Simply put, if we want to predict how well partners will feel they are doing *after* the birth of their first child, our best bet is to look at how they describe key aspects of themselves and their relationship *before* the baby arrives" (p. 4).

In Heming's report, we see some obvious parallels to our framework. First, the importance of prenatal marital structure and/or marital satisfaction as a predictor of the adaptation to parenthood is underscored. Second, there are obvious parallels between the increased gender differentiation reported by the Cowans and our construct of the dominant-submissive marital relationship. Recall that we suggest that some couples negotiate a dominant-submissive relationship during the stage of early relationship formation. According to our hypotheses regarding change along the *Continuum of Marital Competence*, this form of relationship may become openly and severely conflicted under sufficient stress.

In a comparable way, a more egalitarian (highly competent) relationship may be transformed into a dominant-submissive one if the stress is sufficient. It may well be that the Cowans' presentation of increasing gender differentiation between spouses, followed by increasing conflict, is similar to our description of the change from egalitarian to dominant-submissive to conflicted marital structures under stress.

The Cowans' work is thoughtful, rigorous, and most instructive, and but a few questions can be raised about it. One of the questions is their early statement that no pattern of role arrangement and marital communication can be considered ideal or more adaptive than others. I present a different view and would emphasize that their position may reflect something of their primary reliance on self-reported marital satisfaction. I would emphasize that although any type of marital structure may prove satisfying to the spouses, such is not so for their children. Our earlier work suggests that certain types of marital structures are more facilitative of the psychological health of the children and the continued emotional growth of the spouses (Lewis, Beavers, Gossett, & Phillips, 1976; Lewis & Looney, 1983). If such outcome indices are used (and the Cowans appear to use them), then I believe consideration must be given to the possibility that there are certain types of marriages that work better than others—hence, consideration of levels of marital competence.

A second study that relates directly to our concerns in that of Grossman and collaborators (Grossman, Eichler, Winickoff, Anzalone, Gofseyeff, & Sargent, 1980). Like the work of the Cowans, this study is characterized by a multivariate approach and data collection periods in early pregnancy, late pregnancy, early postpartum, and at one year postpartum. The sample includes both couples who are experiencing their first pregnancy and those with previous children. The orienting theoretical position involves the central construct of maturational crisis. The marital dyad is understood as undergoing normative stress and strain in the transition to parenthood brought about by shifts in roles, patterns, and intensity of needs. The crisis presents the couple with the opportunity for growth.

In discussing their findings regarding the course of the pregnancy, the authors note the importance of the quality of the marital relationship. They observe that there is an "infinite variety" of marital styles of coping and that any style can be more or less successful. Some styles do work better, however, by offering more growth-promoting opportunities. They found categorizing the styles of marital coping "incredibly difficult." Their measures of marital quality were derived from standard paper-and-pencil instruments and interviews. They rated the couples on a continuum of traditional to egalitarian relationships on the basis of the division of household tasks. Women in egalitarian marriages had fewer problems during pregnancy.

The authors present data consistent with the view that first-time parents, in contrast to experienced parents, experience the first two months of parenthood as a crisis. The crisis was reflected in the women's increased levels of anxiety and depression, and these were predictable on the basis of prenatal measurements of both the women's ego strengths and the quality of their marriages. Early prenatal measures of the husbands' anxiety levels also predicted the wives' postnatal anxiety and depression. Husbands seemed less caught up in the crisis, and by two months postpartum appeared to see the crisis as a past event. Although wives also tended to speak about it as something in the past, the crisis did not appear to be completely resolved for them at two months. Marital satisfaction was lower at two months than prenatally, although predicted by earlier measurements of marital quality.

The authors note that it is impossible to know the degree of mother-child closeness that is optimal in the early postpartum, but that some of the new mothers had to choose between their newborn children and their husbands.

At one year, the "turmoil and disorganization" of the early postpartum period has passed, and the previously elevated levels of maternal anxiety and depression had subsided for the most part. This recovery from crisis was predicted by the women's prenatal level of emotional integration, socioeconomic status, and level of marital satisfaction. Husbands, generally disappointed with the model of father provided by their fathers, were able to be of greater assistance to their wives if they had earlier reported an image of their own mothers as warm and nurturing.

At one year, the strongest predictors of the state of the marital relationship were the reports of both spouses of the quality of their marriage in the first trimester of pregnancy and at two months postpartum. The authors note that for the first-time parents (but not experienced parents) a very traditional marriage (measured prenatally) was associated with lower levels of marital satisfaction at one year than were egalitarian marriages. Wives with egalitarian marriages did better during pregnancy and were more reciprocal with their infants at two months.

Although almost every wife reported that parenthood produced a negative impact on the marriage, for some couples the effect was a major one. For the children the quality of their parents' marriage was a predictor of their own development at both two months and one year.

A brief review of this rich study does it scant justice. It is an unusually thorough and rigorous piece of work that clearly demonstrates the impact of individual, marital, and contextual variables. From our perspective, we wish that Grossman and her colleagues had included more behavioral and objective observations of the marital relationship rather than relying, for the most part, on each spouse's self-report. From the viewpoint of the impact of marital structure on the transition to parenthood, however, the findings from this study are comparable to those from the Cowans' study. A strong predictor of how well a couple does after parenthood is the nature of their relationship before parenthood. Despite the evidence presented regarding a nearly inevitable crisis in the early months of parenthood, by one year postpartum couples who are doing well in the first trimester of pregnancy were much more likely to be doing well. The suggestion is clear: there is something about the quality or structure of the prenatal marital relationship that influences strongly how the young family will do.

There is also a hint of which aspects of marital structure may be important in the Grossman group's findings regarding traditional and egalitarian marriages. Although there is some doubt from my view that an assessment of marriage can be made solely on the grounds of the division of household tasks, the fact that in some ways wives and children from egalitarian marriages were faring better (if first-time parents) suggests something of our typology and the contrast we will hypothesize between the experiences of those involved in very competent (more egalitarian) marriages and those involved in dominant-submissive (more traditional) marriages.

A third study that relates also to the concerns of our work is that of Shereshefsky and Yarrow (1973). These authors' primary concern was to explore the psychological aspects of first-time mothers' adjustments to pregnancy and the early (first six months) mother-infant relationship. Additionally, they explored the effects of social work counseling on one-half of their sample. Here, as with the Cowans and their colleagues and Grossman et al., a multiple variable framework was used (Cowan et al., 1978; Cowan & Ball, 1981; Cowan & Cowan, 1981; Cowan & Cowan, 1983, Cowan & Cowan, 1985; Cowan & Cowan, 1985a; Grossman et al., 1980).

Their exploration of factors predicting an adaptive adjustment to pregnancy, although not central to our work, is particularly illuminating. There were few significant predictors in the mothers' background data, but the reporting of a positive relationship with a mother seen as warm, empathic, and nurturing did predict successful adaptation to pregnancy. High levels of external stress were associated with less functional maternal adaptation to pregnancy. The authors' finding that women who coped successfully with pregnancy and early parenthood appeared to come to grips with new dimensions of being a woman with increased capacity for nurturance and augmented ego strength is an important observation.

The fathers is this study generally reacted to the pregnancy with symptoms related to increased anxiety and intensified feelings about separation, with an amazing 65 percent experiencing pregnancy-like symptoms of nausea, backache, and gastrointestinal dysfunction.

Several findings relate directly to our concerns. First, 21 percent of the couples were described as manifesting serious marital disharmony at the time of initial prenatal data collection. The authors state that these marriages were marked by an uncertain commitment and thoughts about or attempts to separate. Conflicts regarding the pregnancy itself were incorporated into their ongoing disagreements. This group of couples had the most difficult time with pregnancy and early parenthood. The authors state that serious marital disharmony was the most burdensome and pervasively disruptive stress. Indeed, the two factors that emerge from this study as the strongest predictors of difficulty in pregnancy and early parenthood are maternal ego deficits and serious marital disharmony.

As a whole, these couples manifested increased marital adaptation during pregnancy and decreased marital adaptation during the first six months of parenthood. Marital adaptation was closely correlated with the wives' adaptation to early motherhood. Of particular interest for preventive health measures is the finding that the counselled cohort's level of marital adaptation did not decline during early parenthood, only the marital adaptation levels of the noncounselled group.

A finding that relates to one emerging from our study is the impact of the infant's gender. Selected measures of the mother's personality and her adaptation to pregnancy correlated positively with her maternal competence with girls but not boys. To put this somewhat differently, women with lesser personality strengths and poor adjustments to pregnancy did not do as well with girls as they did with boys.

The authors offer a useful distinction regarding the issue of whether the period of pregnancy and early parenthood is a crisis. They state that if crisis is defined as a stress involving the threat of loss and requiring resources beyond the ordinary, the experience of pregnancy and early parenthood cannot generally be considered a crisis. If, however, crisis is defined as a transitional phase, a turning point, obviously the time of first pregnancy and early parenthood is a crisis.

It is important to note that this early study was not constructed specifically to explore in detail the impact of the marital relationship on pregnancy and early parenthood. The methods of assessing marital adaptation were restricted to paper-and-pencil instruments and individual interviews (self-report). There were no joint interviews or structured observations of marital interaction. By these measures, however, marital disharmony emerged as a strong predictor of adjustment to pregnancy and early parenthood. Couples with dysfunctional and apparently seriously conflicted relationships did not parent as well as couples with more competent relationships.

This study in many respects led the way for more recent longitudinal research. As with the work of the Cowans and Grossman et al., the finding most directly relevant to our concerns is that marital adjustment prior to parenthood influences the couples' experience of parenthood in varied yet decisive ways.

Belsky and his colleagues approach the issue directly and measure stability and change in marriage across the transition to parenthood (Belsky et al., 1983). They used a format of paper-and-pencil instruments, interviews, and home observation. They hypothesized that overall marital quality would decline across the transition and that the decline would reflect, at least in part, the increasing instrumental nature of family life associated with child care. Couples' characterizations of their relationship as a romance would decline along with augmented appraisals of their instrumental partnership. Of particular importance to our interest in marital structure across the transition is their prediction that the changes in the group means for measures of marital quality would be associated with relative stability of ranking among the couples. In other words, couples who scored high or low on measures prenatally would score high or low respectively postnatally.

Their findings support their hypotheses. There are modest but significant unfavorable changes in the marital relationship across the transition. The most dramatic effect was seen at three months postpartum. The wives' marital adjustment was the most sensitive barometer, with striking decreases in their reported sense of marital cohesiveness. Their prediction that the partners' appraisal of the romantic nature of their relationship would decline was confirmed, although statistically this was not significant. There was a significant improvement in their appraisal of the partnership or instrumental aspects of their relationship. Analysis of the relative stability of each couple's ranking relative to all other couples confirmed their hypothesis. Higher-ranked couples prenatally were ranked higher postnatally, and lower-ranked couples were ranked lower throughout the transition. Belsky and his coworkers, therefore, answer the question of whether adding a child affects the marital relationship by stating that it depends on which index of marriage is examined.

Finally, a very different kind of study relates directly to our own. Wenner and her collaborators, all psychoanalysts, offered psychotherapeutic services to pregnant women as the basic data collection procedure for studying the emotional problems of pregnancy (Wenner, Cohen, Weigert, Kvarnes, Ohaneson, & Fearing, 1969). This type of research is less well controlled. The 52 subjects were seen from 12 to 40 times (mean, 23.2 psychotherapeutic interviews), and findings were discussed by the six psychoanalysts comprising the team. Obviously, clinical judgments were contaminated by each researcher's earlier judgments as well as by the opinions of his or her coworkers. An advantage of this type of study, however, is the richness of the data obtained about each subject.

The results are complex but, in general, support the idea that emotional difficulties in pregnancy are directly related to the level of neurosis of the subject. Healthier subjects were more apt to have wanted the pregnancy or accepted it positively and less likely to "need" the pregnancy for defensive purposes. Findings regarding the role of mature versus less mature dependency, the subject's femininity, and the subjects' relationships with parents are also important.

From the perspective of our study, however, the most relevant and fascinating data concerned the subjects' marital relationships. The quality of the marital relationship was a crucial factor affecting the course of the pregnancy. The ability to deal adaptively with pregnancy was present not only in more mature women, but also in some less mature women who had established a satisfactory working relationship with their husbands in which help and support were available and acceptable. Neurotic subjects who had no intensification of their neuroses during pregnancy were very likely (85 percent) to have this type of supportive marriage.

The authors' description of marital types resemble the types described in the preceding chapter as occupying various positions on the *Continuum of Marital Competence*. Subjects who did well were most apt to have "collaborative" or "adult husband-adult wife" relationships. In subjects who had somewhat more difficulty with pregnancy, the marital relationships were dominant-submissive, with one spouse playing a parent role to the other. In the less well integrated subjects who had greater difficulty with pregnancy, the marital type was conflicted. The basic source of the conflict was seen by the investigators as the struggle over who was to be the child and who the parent. Dependency demands were high, and needs remained unsatisfied. Although an increase in dependency needs was observed in all the pregnant women, the needs were associated with regressive phenomena in the more disturbed women with the conflicted, more dysfunctional marriages.

The investigators emphasize the role of conflict over the distribution of power or control as central to the disturbance in the more dysfunctional marriages. Additionally, they report interesting parallels between the subjects' marital relationships and their relationships with parents and their parents' relationship with each other. In particular, the investigators emphasize the importance of the women's adult relationships with their mothers as a strong predictor of the quality of their here-and-now marriages.

Although Wenner's report does not provide data from the early postpartum period, it is important for two reasons. First, the centrality of the quality of the subjects' marriages in predicting the course of pregnancy was not a major hypothesis; rather, its crucial importance became apparent as the study progressed. Second, the investigators' descriptions of marital types bear a close resemblance to those in our earlier work (Lewis et al., 1976; Lewis & Looney, 1983).

These five longitudinal studies offer information regarding the importance of the quality of the marital relationship in the transition to parenthood. In several of the studies, marital quality or satisfaction is one the strongest predictors of how well or poorly early parenthood goes. Each of the studies strongly suggests that couples with more effective relationships before parenthood do better than those with less effective relationships. Our study attempts to clarify and amplify these findings by examining data on the impact of parenthood on couples with various levels of marital competence. Finally, our study adds the crucial dimension of the incorporation of the child to the study of the transition to parenthood and allows the exploration of the relationship between incorporation of the child and changes in the structure of the marital relationship.

PART II

Hypotheses, Methods,
and Findings

PART II

Hypotheses, Methods, and Findings

CHAPTER 4

Hypotheses, Design, and Methods

At the most general level, the hypothesis guiding this project is that there will be a direct relationship between prenatal marital competence and the successful transition to parenthood. Couples with relationship structures rated as highly competent will demonstrate an increased probability of incorporating the child into the family and maintaining the quality of their relationship. As the level of marital competence diminishes, there will be a lessened probability of such a successful transition. In other words, if all other variables (social support, stress, the child's temperament, etc.) are held constant, the more competent the prenatal marital structure, the greater the likelihood of both a successful adaptation to parenthood and the incorporation of the child into the family.

I have focused on two developmental challenges of early parenthood as outcome variables to evaluate the predictive capacity of marital competence. The first challenge involves stability and change in the structure of the parents' relationship over the transition to parenthood. For couples who have achieved a highly competent relationship, the challenge involves maintaining that level of relating in the face of the inevitable strains of late pregnancy, birth, and the first year of parenthood. For couples with less functional relationship patterns, the challenge is to avoid further regression to a more dysfunctional structure or to restructure their relationship to a more functional level.

The position is taken that when changes in marital structure occur they do so in predictable ways. If couples with highly competent marital structures respond to the transition with regressive changes in their relationships, they will do so by becoming more dominant-submissive in their marital structures. Couples with dominant-submissive relationships will move to conflicted structures, and those with chronically conflicted structures will move toward chaos. In comparable ways, improvement in the relationship will involve changes in the relationship structure that follow the above progression in reverse order—that is, a general pattern of chaos and disorganization → conflict → dominance-submission → flexibility.

The second developmental challenge, incorporating the child into the family, is a difficult one to operationalize and I have been unable to find published data that point the way. In our study, a child is considered to be incorporated into the family if he or she becomes a participant in the family's recurring patterns of activity and affective exchange. Successful incorporation will be reflected by patterns of activity that do not exclude any participants or involve unpleasant affects.

Three different and complementary approaches to measurement were used. The first measure involved systematic observations of each spouse's parenting skills. This is based on the belief that sensitive parenting is an important index of the extent to which parents are capable of meeting the challenges of new parenthood, and, thus, one way to index their success in incorporating the child into the family. The thesis is that the mutual caretaking and nurturing that occur in some marriages contribute to sensitive parenting. In effect, I postulate that spouses who are able to be sensitive and nurturing with each other are developing skills necessary for effective parenting.

The second approach to operationalizing the incorporation of the child into the family was the measurement of attachment relationships in each infant-parent dyad. A standard approach to the measurement of attachment behavior was used (Ainsworth, Blehar, Waters, & Wall, 1978). The hypothesis is that the level of prenatal marital competence will predict the quality of the infant-parent attachment. Here, as with the measurement of parenting skills, the prediction is that marital competence predicts secure attachment, and does so independently of the psychological health of each spouse. To the extent that individual psychological health and marital competence are related, it is necessary to test whether any relation between marital competence and some outcome is due to the marital structure per se or due to the individual health of the individuals involved in the relationship.

The premise for this prediction of a relationship between marital competence and infant-parent attachment is that the construct of marital competence is thought to measure both connectedness and autonomy. Highly competent couples who have evolved relationships characterized by high levels of both have created a dyadic system in which the fostering of the infant's secure attachment is more likely. Couples whose relationship is characterized by greater interpersonal distance will be less likely to have created a system in which secure attachment is as probable. Couples with fused or symbiotic relationships will also be less likely to facilitate secure infant-parent attachments because of their insensitivity to differences and their strong need for sameness. I believe this can lead to failures in the capacity to read sensitively a child's needs and moods, thereby diminishing the likelihood of secure attachment.

The third approach to the measurement of incorporation of the child into the family is an attempt to move beyond dyadic measurements (parent sensitivity to child and infant-parent attachment relationships) and to observe and quantify triadic interactions. Rating scales were constructed to measure patterns of activity and affect during a play session videotaped at home which included both parents and their one-year-old infant. In this procedure, raters scored the predominant activity pattern (both parents playing jointly with child, parents taking turns playing with child, only one parent playing with child, etc.) and scored the degree of pleasurable affect, its level of intensity, and the degree to which it was shared by all three participants. The premise was that the nature of the parents' prenatal relationship should influence their capacity to share pleasurable time and activity with their child. Couples with more dysfunctional relationships will be less likely to be jointly and pleasurably involved with their child.

These hypotheses involve the predictive capacity of a general, overall index of marital quality, marital competence. Yet the possibility exists that specific aspects of the marital structure may be better predictors for particular developmental transitions. Reiss and his coworkers, for example, discuss the "weakness of strong bonds"; that is, competent families may do well dealing with acute illness, but do less well in dealing with chronic illness as, for example, a family member undergoing dialysis for end-stage renal disease (Reiss, Gonzalez, & Kramer, 1986). This provocative work deals with severe stress (not family developmental transitions), but it can be used to construct hypotheses regarding the transition to parenthood and other developmental transitions. Such hypotheses suggest that each developmental transition challenges different aspects of the family's structure. Thus, a global measure of marital or family competence may not predict successful adaptation to new stages of the family life cycle; rather, different characteristics may be better predictors for each stage of the cycle. In this regard, Combrinck-Graham's (1985) theory of family development hypothesizes that success in early parenthood could be predicted on the basis of closeness and intimacy in the prenatal marital relationship. During late adolescence and early adulthood, however, successful adaptation would more likely be predicted by family characteristics that predict separateness and the capacity for autonomous functioning.

The predictions for couples with various levels of marital competence were as follows.

THE HIGHLY COMPETENT MARRIAGE

The prediction for these couples was for a relatively smooth transition to parenthood. I predicted that these couples deal with the inevitable developmental strains and stresses without alteration in the basic structure of their relationship. They move through late pregnancy, birth, and the first year of parenthood all the while maintaining a relationship structure characterized by high levels of closeness, significant individual autonomy, the capacity for intimate communication, high levels of commitment, and shared power.

Couples with highly competent marriages are also predicted to demonstrate successful incorporation of the child into the family as reflected by all three measures: parenting skills, the quality of the infant's attachments, and direct observation of triadic behavior.

Couples with this type of relationship can, however, have difficulty with the transition to parenthood if stressful external circumstances occur. Job loss, the death of a close family member, the birth of a seriously defective child are examples. Under such circumstances I hypothesize that some couples' coping mechanisms will be overwhelmed and a crisis experienced, with the likelihood of change in the structure of their relationship in the direction of increasing distance, dominance and submission, and, ultimately, severe conflict. In addition to the alterations in marital structure, these circumstances are associated with a reduced likelihood of successful incorporation of the child into the family.

THE COMPETENT BUT PAINED MARRIAGE

In earlier work with families containing adolescent children, the competent but pained parental relationships appeared by history to be long-term structures. With some exceptions, the wife was the chronic pursuer. In the current sample of younger couples, the length of the marriage averaged 3.5 years in contrast to 20 years for the earlier samples. Are the younger couples in this sample as fixed in the competent but pained structure as the couples in earlier samples appeared to be? Are some of these couples capable of significant improvement in their relationship as part of sharing parenthood for the first time? Recall that this type of marital structure is considered to be intermediate between highly competent and clearly dysfunctional structures. These couples have many strengths, and if any subgroup of our sample is able to improve their relationship structure as a consequence of the transition, it should be this subgroup.

At a general level, there is a high likelihood that couples with competent but pained marital structures experience the transition to parenthood without crisis and in a relatively smooth manner. For most such couples, the anticipation is for no change in the structure of their relationships and a good probability that the child would be successfully incorporated into the family. The qualifications regarding incorporation of the child were based upon the anticipation that there is high likelihood that the wife (more frequently the dissatisfied pursuer) finds sought-for closeness in her relationship with the child and is less dissatisfied with the absence of closeness in the marital relationship. From this perspective it is anticipated that both wife and husband feel better about their relationship during the early years of parenthood, perhaps before the child's normative push for separateness and autonomy intervenes.

In a minority of cases the husband is the dissatisfied pursuer. I hypothesize a similar sequence insofar as circumstances allow the development of a close father-child relationship.

In short, for the competent but pained subgroup, the hypothesis was that if the structure of the marital relationship remains constant the child will be placed very early in life in a substitutive role. Although the long-range implications of this process may be questionable for child, marriage, and family, the short-term implications may seem positive.

A second set of possibilities is less likely. These involve the idea that the experience of closeness in the mother-child or father-child relationship increases rather than decreases the dissatisfaction with the marital relationship. This could lead to increasing distance and conflict and a regressive change in the structure of the marital relationship. Such events are predicted to be more likely when stressful outside circumstances are also present. A difficult child or a job change may be enough stress to produce regression in couples with a competent but pained relationship.

THE DOMINANT-SUBMISSIVE MARRIAGE

This type of marital structure involves a clear but complementary, skewed distribution of power. If conflict is ongoing and open, the marital structure is considered to be in the conflicted category. The hypotheses presented here, therefore, apply only to relationship structures in which the way power is shared is broadly acceptable to both participants. Such relationship structures are understood as dysfunctional because in our early studies such parental relationships were associated with an increased probability of clinical syndromes in adolescent family members.

The hypothesis for this type of marital structure is that of an increased likelihood of crisis experienced with the transition to parenthood, with change in the structure of the relationship most likely of a regressive nature. This prediction is based on the premise that the rigidity of such structures makes dealing with the unpredictable more difficult. Such couples, therefore, may be particularly vulnerable when complications of delivery and early parenthood are experienced. I predict also an increased probability of difficulty in the incorporation of the child into the family.

The prediction of a difficult transition is made independently of which spouse is the dominant in the relationship. The magnitude of the power differential is the factor that is predicted to influence the probability of a difficult transition. In marriages in which one spouse is in charge of every aspect of the marriage, the submissive spouse may be so childlike and dependent that the early demands of parenting may overwhelm his or her resources. This pattern increases the probability of crisis and structural change and diminishes the likelihood of successful incorporation of the child into the family. If structural change occurs, it will be predictable: Regression will involve intensifying conflict and disorganization; improvement will be toward increased egalitarianism.

THE CONFLICTED MARRIAGE

Because severely dysfunctional, chaotic couples do not often volunteer for family research projects, the anticipation was that couples with chronically conflicted marital structures would be the most dysfunctional subgroup in this sample. The basic hypothesis was, therefore, that, more than any other type, couples with this form of relationship undergo stormy, difficult transitions and that there is a higher probability of failure to incorporate the child into the family.

I predict that couples experiencing crises and structural changes would change toward increasing conflict and disintegration of the relationship. Conflict may decrease in some such couples, however, when a close parent-child coalition excludes the other parent. As suggested in the possibilities for the transition in the dominant-submissive couples, the long-term implications of these parent-child coalitions may not bode well for the child's development, but in the short run the early establishment of a "perverse" triangle may reduce the conflict in the family system (Haley, 1981). In general, constant parental strife is considered to be a potential deterrent to the kind of sensitive parenting and effective, pleasurable sharing of parenthood upon which successful incorporations are based.

THE SEVERELY DYSFUNCTIONAL MARRIAGE

I did not anticipate that couples with this form of marriage would volunteer for this type of family research. Therefore, I could only speculate that such couples would be most apt to have serious and profound difficulties with the transition to parenthood. Regardless of whether the basic marital structure is symbiotic or dominated by a severely disturbed, reality-distorting spouse, the rigidity, disorganization, failure to maintain interpersonal boundaries, resistance to change, imperviousness to the surroundings, and reliance on primitive intrapsychic and interpersonal mechanisms are so severe that sensitive parenting appears highly unlikely. It might well be that a child would be incorporated into a symbiotic marital system, not as an object of independent regard, but rather as an extension or projection of some part of one or both parents' self-systems.

In terms of the structure of the marital system itself, I have been impressed clinically with the difficulty involved in facilitating greater degrees of individuation in each spouse. These marital and family systems are remarkably resistant to change, and my speculation is that such marital systems would be most likely to experience the transition to parenthood without change.

In summary, the central hypothesis is that competence in resolving the tasks of early marriage plays a significant role in the transition to parenthood. Couples with more competent marital structures generally will have a relatively smooth transition. Couples with rigid dysfunctional marital structures will be more likely to suffer crisis. Some of these couples will experience a sudden transformation in marital structure, while in others the marital relationship will dissolve. The changes in marital satisfaction for couples with different types of marital structures were also seen as predictable and dependent, in part, on the circumstances outlined above. Finally, I hypothesized that when the transition to parenthood involved a basic change in the structure of the marital relationship, the structural change will be predictable and follow the flexible $\rightleftarrows$ rigid $\rightleftarrows$ chaotic format.

DESIGN

This investigation of how competent families develop over time uses data from a longitudinal study with a multimethod, multimeasure design. Couples were enlisted before the birth of their first child. Data were collected during the second trimester of the pregnancy, three months after the birth, and one year after the birth. These couples are still being followed at later time periods, but only data from these early time periods are reported here.

Extensive interviews, observations, questionnaires, and standardized personality measures were used at each data collection period to obtain information concerning the major areas of interest. These are: the parental relationship, sources of stress and support at each time period, the parent-child relationships, the new triadic system, and the development of the child.

The sample was limited to white, middle-class couples where neither husband nor wife had any previous children and who gave birth to infants considered normal and healthy. Because only 40 couples were enlisted, the demographic characteristics of the sample were relatively homogeneous in order to increase the statistical power to detect significant differences in relation to the constructs examined. The data reported here were collected between June, 1982 and February, 1985.

Subjects

Forty couples were recruited from the patients of 23 obstetricians at Baylor University Medical Center in Dallas, Texas. An attempt was made to contact all couples who fit the project's criteria in the practices of these obstetricians. Of those contacted, 74 percent agreed to participate. Of the initial sample of 40 couples, two couples dropped out of the study before completing the initial round of data collection. On the basis of demographic data, these two couples were not significantly different from the rest of the participants. It seemed apparent, however, that they had relatively more marital and personal difficulties than did most of the other couples and, in that sense, the loss was not random. All of the 38 other couples remained in the study through the one-year postnatal data collection period.

At the time of enlistment, the mean length of marriage for the couples was 3.5 years. The average age of the wives was 27.3 years, with a range from 18-35. The average age of the husbands was 29.4 years, with a range of 21-42. The mean family income fell in the $35,000-$39,999 range. The mean education for husbands was 15.8 years and for wives 15.5 years. Using the Hollingshead (1975) Four-Factor Index of Social Class, couple scores on social class ranged from 32-66, with a mean of 52.4. Forty-eight percent of the couples were in a major business and professional category; 42 percent in a medium business, minor professional, and technical category; and 10 percent in a working class category. Thus, the sample appears to represent lower- to upper-middle-class white families in an urban area.

All but one of the 38 infants born to these couples were full-term or near-term and healthy newborns. One female infant was born six weeks prematurely, but as her prognosis was for healthy, normal development, the family was not excluded from the study.

Procedure

After obtaining couples' names from the obstetricians, each couple was contacted by the Director of the project, first by a letter explaining the project and then by a follow-up phone call. In the phone call, questions were answered and more detail on what participation would involve was provided. If the couple agreed to participate, the first of two prenatal visits was scheduled.

Prenatal visits. In the first visit, the Director of the project went to the couple's home, answered any questions, and again described the project and its requirements. After they were fully informed of the implications of participating, the husband and wife were asked to sign a consent form to participate. Each spouse was then interviewed privately in a separate part of the home, while the other spouse filled out questionnaires and personality measures. The interviews lasted from two to three hours, were tape-recorded, and later transcribed. Whether husband or wife was interviewed first was determined by a coin toss, except in a few cases when their schedules dictated that one go first. At the end of this visit, a second visit in the laboratory at the research foundation was scheduled within the following two weeks. The couple was informed at this time concerning what was involved in that second visit.

In the second prenatal visit, couples came to the laboratory and were interviewed together by one of the research assistants, who was usually a doctoral student in clinical psychology. This interview lasted from one to 1.5 hours and was videotaped. After the interview, the couple was left alone in the same room to undertake structured marital interactional tasks. This procedure also was videotaped. An audiotape in the room gave the theme of each task and told the couple when to begin and when to end each of four tasks. The instructions given to the couple were that they were to have a discussion as they would if they were alone at home in their own living room. The video-taped interview preceding the marital interaction tasks provided some desensitization to being videotaped and allowed the couple to become comfortable with the room.

Three-month visits. Contact was made with the couples in the hospital at the birth of the child and again when the child was three months old. Data from the hospital visit are not reported at this time. Prior to the three-month visit, each couple was sent a description of what the three-month visit would entail.

During the second postnatal month, three visits were scheduled with each couple to occur in the two weeks after the child turned three months. In the first visit, a home visitor spent a morning with the mother and child during which first the Bayley Scales of Infant Development (mental and motor) were administered and the Infant Behavior Record was completed. The mother held the infant on her lap for part of the mental portion of the Bayley Scales. The mothers were instructed that they could observe the administration of the Bayley Scales, but must not interact or be involved in the administration except on items where the researcher gave specific instructions for the mother's involvement (for example, on the item where one sees if the infant shows recognition of the mother).

Following this, an informal observation and interview period occurred so that the home visitor could complete the H.O.M.E. observation interview for the assessment of the environment (Caldwell & Bradley, 1987). This interview involved questioning the mother as well as unstructured observations of the home (including play areas and the child's room) and observations of the mother-child relationship. At the end of this visit, the appointment for the next visit was confirmed, and more information was given concerning what would happen at that visit.

The second visit occurred in the laboratory. Each parent was interviewed individually for approximately two hours in a comfortable setting. Interviews were again audiotaped and later transcribed. While one parent was interviewed, the other was administered the Wechsler Adult Intelligence Scale-Revised (WAIS-R). After the interviews and testing, the parents again engaged in videotaped, structured, marital interaction tasks similar to the one described in the prenatal period.

In a third visit in the home, each parent was videotaped in separate 15-minute semistructured interactions with his or her infant, followed by 15 minutes of interaction among all three family members (45 minutes of interaction in total). For these observations, the camera was fixed in the family's living room so that the parent and child, and later both parents and child, could be left alone. We assumed that the parents would feel more comfortable if they were unobserved except by the camera in their own home. Parents were told what constituted camera range and were asked to stay within camera range. They also were asked to do "whatever you would normally do with the infant when you are alone with the infant at this time of day." Several special microphones were used to catch sound in various parts of the room so that the sounds of the interaction were well recorded. After the parent-child interactions, the couple was interviewed together. The interview lasted about 45 minutes. At this visit parents were also given a series of questionnaires and personality measures to complete.

One-year visits. Between the three-month and the one-year visits, all couples were sent a letter explaining what would be involved in the one-year visits and when they would be scheduled. Within a month after the baby's first birthday, three visits were scheduled. In the first visit, a home visitor spent a morning with the mother and child. First, the Bayley Scales of Infant Development (mental and motor) were administered and the Infant Behavior Record completed. The mothers held the babies for the mental portion of the Bayley Scales, but were instructed to say nothing and be as uninvolved as possible. After the Bayley Scales, the H.O.M.E. observation interview for the assessment of the environment was again completed as described for the three-month visit.

In a second visit in the home, the parents and children were observed in 15-minute interactions with each parent-child dyad and a 15-minute interaction of the whole family. These interactions were videotaped, but a screen was set up around the camera so that the camera could follow the actions of the parents and children. The camera was set up in a doorway or opening to the room or a corner of the room so that a physical barrier could be constructed between the camera and the family and the individual operating the camera could be hidden from view as much as possible. This was necessary because one-year olds are curious and the camera was an object of interest to them. Videotaping was begun in each case after the child had become acclimated to the presence of the barrier around the camera. After the parent-child interactions, audiotaped interviews were conducted with each parent privately in separate areas of the home. At this visit, parents were also given a series of questionnaires and personality measures to complete.

In a third visit, parents and children came to the laboratory. By a toss of a coin, one of the parents and the child were involved in a videotaped strange situation procedure (Ainsworth et al., 1978). After the strange situation, the couple was left alone in a room to complete additional marital interaction tasks similar to those described at the prenatal and three-month time periods.

In a fourth visit, occurring from 7 to 10 weeks after the third visit, a second strange situation procedure was conducted in the laboratory with the child and the other parent.

Measures

Demographic information. Each spouse completed a questionnaire giving basic demographic information, including occupation, education, age, length of marriage, length of employment, income, religious affiliation, age at pregnancy, birth order, whether parents were living and, if not, cause of death. Complete demographic information was obtained in the prenatal period, while question- naires asking whether there were any changes in jobs, addresses, education level and so on were given at the three-month and one-year periods.

Individual interviews. Audiotaped individual interviews were conducted with each spouse at the prenatal, three-month, and one-year periods (see Appendix 1a, 1b, & 1c). The interviews were semistructured — that is, a series of questions were constructed to obtain information on variables of interest, and interviewers were trained to follow-up and explore areas where responses suggested that information of value lay beyond the initial answers to the questions.

The interviews explored the areas of the subject's work, marriage, friendships, support networks, family of origin, and perception of self and individual functioning. In addition, after the birth of the child, the parent-child relationship, the child's development, attitudes toward the child and the parenting experi- ence and parental employment were explored.

Marital interviews. Videotaped marital interviews were conducted prenatally. Couples were asked about how their relationship developed, feelings about the pregnancy, expectations of parenthood, religious issues, and plans for the future. At three months after the birth of the child, a videotaped interview with both parents explored their responses to being parents, how roles and responsibilities were divided, the amount of conflict and disruption in the marital relationship, and plans for more children (see Appendix 2a & 2b).

Marital interactions. At the prenatal, three-month postnatal, and one-year postnatal periods, couples participated in a videotaped marital interaction. For these interactions couples were in a familiar, living-room-like setting in the laboratory and were asked to discuss a series of issues which were presented by an audiotape in the room (see Appendix 3). Eight minutes were given for each issue, and the tape instructed the couple when to begin and when to end each discussion. At least one of the discussion tasks required the couples to resolve some disagreement, while others required that they speak with each other concerning private and sometimes painful aspects of their marriage. In this way, we obtained information concerning interactional processes in couples.

Parent-infant interactions. Interactions between each parent and the infant were videotaped for 15 minutes in the home, followed by a 15-minute videotape of the family triad at both three months and one year. These interactions were semistructured in that parents had to stay in one room with the child, but they were given instructions to do whatever was normally done with that child at that time. For the one-year interactions, a standardized set of toys was provided which served to structure the interaction somewhat. The toys included a ball, a doll, a hammering toy, an airplane, and a plastic, take-apart iron.

Infant-parent attachment. Using Ainsworth's Strange Situation Procedure, the security of the infant-parent attachment was assessed at one year for each infant-parent dyad (Ainsworth et al., 1978). This procedure was designed to index individual differences in the quality of infant-mother attachment and has been used to index differences in infant-father attachment as well (Main & Weston, 1981). The procedure consists of a series of three-minute episodes designed to stress the infant gradually. It begins with the infant and parent in an unfamiliar room equipped with attractive toys; this is followed in turn by the entrance of an unfamiliar woman, the departure of the parent, the parent's return, the unfamiliar woman's departure, the parent's second departure, and the parent's return. Of particular interest in this procedure is the child's behavior upon reunion with the parent.

Individual adult measures. A variety of measures of adult personality and functioning were used in the study at each time period. The personality measures used were ones whose psychometric properties are well-known and for which extensive information concerning reliability and validity is available. Therefore, these are listed and referenced without discussion of reliability and validity studies. These personality measures were employed so that we could try to understand what is considered a reciprocal relationship between adult personality and functioning and adult relationships and experiences. In other words, we assume that individuals who are psychologically healthier and function better are able to form better relationships with others, and that those relationships support better psychological health and functioning over time. Moreover, it was assumed that those with better psychological health weather adult-life transitions better, and that life transitions can contribute in turn to adult psychological growth and maturity. To understand these important relationships, a range of measures of adult personality and functioning were employed to capture the critical aspects of this important area. The measures used included:

1. *The California Psychological Inventory* (Gough, 1975) at the prenatal period.
2. *The Beck Depression Inventory* (Beck, Ward, Mendelson, Mock, & Erbaugh, 1961) at the prenatal, three-month, and one-year time periods.
3. *The Spielberger State-Trait Anxiety Measure* (Speilberger, Gorsuch, & Lushsens, 1970) at the prenatal and three-month time periods.
4. *The Personal Adjustment Scale of the Adjective Checklist* (Gough & Heilbrun, 1965) at the prenatal, three-month, and one-year time periods. Each spouse completed the Personal Adjustment Scale once for *self* and once for *spouse.*
5. *The Locus of Control* (Paulhus & Christie, 1981) at the prenatal, three-month, and one-year time periods.
6. *The Sentence Completion Test* of ego development (Loevinger & Wessler, 1970; Loevinger, Wessler, & Redmore, 1970) at the prenatal and one-year time periods.
7. *The Wechsler Adult Intelligence Scale-Revised (WAIS-R)* was administered to the husband and wife at the three-month time period.

In addition, a series of questionnaires were given to the husband and wife individually to assess levels of stress, support systems, family role divisions and satisfactions, relationships to families of origin, and marital satisfaction. The measures used included the following:

1. *The Life Experiences Survey* (Sarason, Johnson, & Siegel, 1978) was used to measure stress at the prenatal and three-month time periods.
2. *The Social Network Survey* (Margolis, undated) was used to measure each individual's network of family and friends, the amount of support he or she felt from family and friends, satisfaction with support, support from the work environment and work relationships, and feelings about the neighborhood environment. This measure was used at the prenatal period, and a shortened version was used at the three-month period.
3. *The Family Role Survey* (Gallagher, undated) is a survey developed to assess how roles are divided between spouses, how individual spouses would prefer they be divided, and how satisfied individual spouses are with the divisions. This measure was used at the prenatal, three-month, and one-year time periods.

4. *The Marital Relationships and Marital Problems Inventory (MRI)* (Locke & Wallace, 1959) is a widely used measure of marital adaptation and satisfaction which also includes an inventory of marital problems in a number of areas. This measure was used at the prenatal period, with the marital problems inventory repeated at the three-month and one-year time periods.

5. *The Family of Origin Questionnaire.* At Time 1 subjects rated aspects of their childhood relationships with both their mothers and fathers in a questionnaire adapted from one used by Shereshefsky and Yarrow (1973) to obtain data about relationships with parents during childhood and adolescence (see Appendix 4).

Clinician's Summary Assessment of Individual Psychological Health

A summary rating of each spouse's psychological health was made at Time 1. The rating was made by a senior clinical psychologist on the basis of each subject's responses to nine standard psychological measures and the psychologist's interpretation of each subject's California Psychological Inventory profile (CPI) (Gough, 1975). The nine psychological tests were State Anxiety-Trait Anxiety (Speilberger et al, 1970), the Cornell Medical Index (Brodman, Erdmann, & Wolff, 1949), Life Stress (Sarason, Johnson, & Siegel, 1978), Beck Depression Inventory (Beck et al., 1961), Locus of Control (Paulhus & Christie, 1981), Marital Relationship Inventory (Locke & Wallace, 1959), the Personal Adjustment Scale of the Adjective Checklist (Gough & Heilburn, 1965), the Shipley-Hartford Vocabulary Scale (Shipley, 1940), and Ego Development (Loevinger et al. 1970; Loevinger & Wessler, 1970).

The de-identified scores on the nine psychological tests (10 counting state and trait anxiety scores as two tests) were categorized into three levels: "1" for above average psychological health, "2" for average psychological health, and "3" for below average psychological health. For each subject a composite score was constructed by summing the 10 test scores. An individual, for example, whose test scores were all above average would receive a score of "10," and an individual with all scores below average would receive a score of "30." The subjects' scores ranged from 15 to 27.

In a separate procedure, the psychologist sorted the de-identified CPI profiles into four groups according to his interpretation of their levels of psychological health. The final rating of each subject's level of psychological health was made by combining the summed ratings of the 10 test scores and the interpretation of the CPI profiles. The CPI profiles were used in this way to validate the summed test score ratings. Five levels of individual psychological

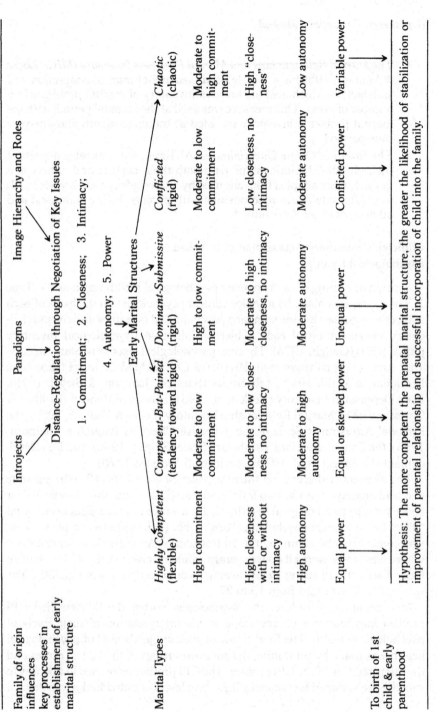

	Early Marital Structures				
Marital Types	*Highly Competent* (flexible)	*Competent-But-Pained* (tendency toward rigid)	*Dominant-Submissive* (rigid)	*Conflicted* (rigid)	*Chaotic* (chaotic)
	High commitment	Moderate to low commitment	High to low commitment	Moderate to low commitment	Moderate to high commitment
	High closeness with or without intimacy	Moderate to low closeness, no intimacy	Moderate to high closeness, no intimacy	Low closeness, no intimacy	High "closeness"
	High autonomy	Moderate to high autonomy	Moderate autonomy	Moderate autonomy	Low autonomy
	Equal power	Equal or skewed power	Unequal power	Conflicted power	Variable power

Family of origin
influences
key processes in
establishment of early
marital structure

Introjects   Paradigms   Image Hierarchy and Roles

Distance-Regulation through Negotiation of Key Issues

1. Commitment;   2. Closeness;   3. Intimacy;

4. Autonomy;   5. Power

To birth of 1st
child & early
parenthood

Hypothesis: The more competent the prenatal marital structure, the greater the likelihood of stabilization or improvement of parental relationship and successful incorporation of child into the family.

Figure 1. Factors involved in establishing marital structure.

health were thus formed with "1" representing the healthiest level, "3" the average level, and "5" the most dysfunctional level.

By using this procedure, 9 subjects were rated as "1," 4 subjects as "2," 44 subjects as "3," 13 subjects as "4," and 8 subjects as "5."

The Process of Rating Marital Competence

In the ratings of marital competence at Time 1, the rater viewed 32 minutes of videotaped marital interactions using the Beavers-Timberlawn Family Evaluation Scales (see Appendix 5). The rater also read the transcripts of each spouse's semistructured individual interview (45-120 minutes) and the transcript of the semistructured marital interview (90-150 minutes). He or she also read each spouse's Marital Relationship Inventory (MRI), Role Survey, and the ratings of support from the spouse made when each completed a Social Network Survey. The rater was blind to all other data about these couples.

At three months and at one year, the same procedure was used to rate marital competence with the exception that no marital interview was administered at one year.

Using these interviews, observations, and self-report data, the rater scored each couple on scales differentiating various levels of commitment, closeness, psychological intimacy, autonomy, and power and then made an overall rating of the level of marital competence on a 10-point *Continuum of Marital Competence* Scale (see Appendix 6a & 6b).

OVERVIEW

Longitudinal family research is complex. Before beginning to examine the data from this early stage of our research, the reader may be clearer about the basic design of the project if it is presented in schematic form. This is done in Figure 1.

CHAPTER 5

Correlates of Marital Competence

Before the data directly relevant to the central hypothesis stated in the preceding chapter are described, it is useful to present correlation data regarding the construct of marital competence, the variable from which we attempted to predict various outcomes in the transition to parenthood.

At the time of initial data collection, individual and dyadic data were collected from each couple. Some of these data were used in arriving at the ratings of marital competence; other data were not used in this way and can, therefore, be used in examining the correlates of marital competence. In presenting these correlates I hope to illuminate the construct of marital competence. The data will be presented first as they pertain to the individual characteristics of the husbands and wives, and second as they relate to characteristics of the couples as units.

First, however, Table 1 presents the distribution of marital competence ratings in this volunteer sample.

Eight of the couples' relationship structures were rated as highly competent, 13 as competent but pained, 10 as dominant-submissive, complementary, and seven as conflicted. There were no couples rated at the severely dysfunctional end of the *Continuum of Marital Competence*, a finding that is not surprising. This distribution of marital competence scores is similar to those found in earlier studied samples of research volunteer families.

An earlier version of the chapter was published in *Family Process, 27,* June, 1988. Reprinted with permission of *Family Process.*

Table 1
Distribution of Marital Competence Scores at Time 1

1	2	3	4	5	6	7	8	9	10
Highly Competent		Competent but Pained		Dominant-Submissive, Complementary		Conflicted		Severely Dysfunctional	
8		13		10		7		0	

$n = 38$

Table 2
Marital Competence:
Correlations with Demographic Data

	Correlation Coefficients (rs)		
	Wife	Husband	Significance (p)
Ages	−.25	−.11	N.S.
Length of Marriage	−.19		N.S.
Birth Order	.05	−.03	N.S.
Number of Siblings	−.19	−.07	N.S.
Socioeconomic Status	.35		.03

A second issue concerns whether certain of the demographic data correlate with the ratings of marital competence. As can be noted in Table 2, the only significant correlation was with socioeconomic status. This modest correlation indicated that greater competence in the marriage was associated with higher socioeconomic status.

An interesting issue is whether measures of individual psychological health are correlated with marital competence. Several theories of marital relationships emphasize the compositional aspects of marital quality; that is, healthy persons are attracted to and marry other healthy persons, whereas less well integrated persons are also attracted to each other. Relevant data from this sample are presented in Table 3.

All the correlations were positive. Six of the seven measures correlated significantly for wives, and three of seven for husbands. For wives but not husbands, both depression and anxiety were lower with more competent

Table 3
Marital Competence: Correlations with Measures of
Individual Psychological Health

Measures	Correlations**** (r)	
	Wives	Husbands
Personal Adjustment Adjective Check List	.42**	.52***
Ego Development (Loevinger)	.38*	.30
Locus of Control (Paulhus)	.21	.35*
Depression (Beck)	.41**	.06
Anxiety, State (Speilberger)	.55***	.27
Anxiety, Trait (Speilberger)	.32*	.28
Clinician's Summed Assessment 5-Point Level of Adjustment Scale	.42**	.62***

*p < .05
**p < .01
***p < .001
****Adjusted where necessary for direction of scales.

marriages. Locus of control was more internalized among men the more competent their marriages.

These findings suggest a relationship of moderate magnitude between marital competence and individual psychological health. These correlational data, however, do not illuminate the nature of the influence (whether psychological health influences marital competence or vice versa), but it is likely that the influence is reciprocal.

Table 4 demonstrates another way of presenting the relationship between marital competence and individual psychological health.

For both husbands and wives involved in marriages rated as highly competent, there was a high probability of high levels of ego development. For spouses involved in clearly dysfunctional marriages, there was about an equal probability of higher and lower levels of ego development. Twenty-eight of the 44 spouses with higher levels of ego development were involved in marriages rated as highly competent, and five of the 19 spouses with lower levels of ego development were involved in marriages rated as highly competent. These data suggest that the relationship between marital competence and individual psychological health is stronger at higher levels of marital competence than it is at lower levels of marital competence.

Several null findings are of interest. First, there were no significant correlations between marital competence and individual IQ. Second, there were no significant correlations between marital competence and either husbands' or wives' prenatal life stress scores.

Table 4
Marital Competence and Psychological Health:
Levels of Ego Development

	Ego Development	
Marital Competence	High (6, 7, 8)	Low (4, 5)
High (1, 2, 3,)		
Wives	14	3
Husbands	14	2
Low (6, 7, 8)		
Wives	9	6
Husbands	7	8

Significant differences for husbands ($x^2 = 4.19$, $p < .05$)

Table 5
Marital Satisfaction and Marital Interaction Ratings

		Marital Relationship Inventory	
Beavers-Timberlawn Marital Interaction	*n*	Husbands	Wives*
High Scores (1, 2)	12	107	111
Low Scores (5-8)	11	101	101

*$t = 2.46$, $11df$, $p < .05$

We could not examine the correlations between marital competence and marital satisfaction scores because the latter were part of the data used in establishing the level of marital competence. We could, however, examine the correlations between marital satisfaction scores and observers' ratings of the videotaped marital interactions. These measurements were obtained independently and compare an insider perspective and an outsider perspective on the marital relationship. This comparison is presented in Table 5.

Both husbands and wives involved in marital interactions rated as highly competent reported greater satisfaction from their marriages than did spouses in marriages rated as dysfunctional. The differences were modest, however, and were significant only for wives. These findings are interpreted to suggest that, for the most part, spouses' ratings of their marital satisfaction and observers' ratings of marital quality reflect different perspectives of the marital relationship.

Another issue involves the relationship of marital competence to the spouses' values. One aspect of this relationship is presented in Table 6.

Table 6
Marital Competence and Agreement on Values*

Husband & Wife Correlation		n	Mean Marital Competence
A. $r \geq 70$		10	3.0
B. $r = .35 - .69$		20	4.7
C. $r = < .35$		9	5.0
A & B	$t = 2.19$ 28df	$p < .05$	
A & C	$t = 2.18$ 19df	$p < .05$	
B & C	$t = .32$ 27df	N.S.	

*Rokeach Value Survey, Terminal Values $n = 39$
Highest ranked (family security, self-respect, happiness, wisdom, and mature love) and
lowest ranked values (world of peace, equality, world of beauty, social recognition, and
national security) do not differ significantly for husbands and wives.

Table 7
Patterns of Spouse Psychological Health and
Marital Competence

Spouses' Pattern of Psychological Health	n	Mean Marital Competence
1. High-High	24	3.63
2. High-Low	8	5.00
3. Low-Low	6	6.33

1 versus 2 and 3
$t = 2.96$, 36df, $p < .01$

Several theories of marital structure emphasize the role of the spouses' agreement regarding basic values as an important variable in facilitating the relationship. The data presented in Table 6 suggest that couples for whom there is a high level of agreement on their values (ranked independently by husband and wife) are more apt to be involved in marriages rated as more competent. It is not possible to know from these data how much agreement about values facilitates a competent marriage and how much a competent marriage promotes agreement on values. Undoubtedly both pathways operate, and premarital value rankings would be necessary to understand better the nature of influence.

When the focus is turned to the psychological health of both spouses, with the couple as the unit of analysis, a different perspective becomes apparent.

Table 8
Patterns of Spouse Psychological Health and
Types of Marital Structure

Spouses' Pattern of Psychological Health	Levels of Marital Competence			
Marital Competence Ratings	Highly Competent (1 - 2)	Competent but Pained (3 - 4)	Dominant-Submissive Complementary (5 - 6)	Conflicted (7 - 8)
1. High-High	6	12	5	1
2. High-Low	2	1	2	3
3. Low-Low	0	0	3	3

$$x^2 = 15.4$$
$$p < .02$$

As can be noted in Table 7, 24 of the 38 couples involved two spouses with average or higher levels of psychological health (high-high), eight couples involved one spouse with average or higher psychological health and one spouse with lower than average psychological health (high-low), and six couples were comprised of two spouses with lower than average levels of psychological health (low-low). The difference in mean marital competence scores between the 24 high-high couples and the 14 other couples was significant. It is also clear that 30 of the 38 couples were comprised of spouses with equivalent levels of psychological health or, in different terms, 60 of the 76 subjects were married to spouses of approximately equal levels of psychological health.

A second set of analyses provided, however, a somewhat different perspective. As can be noted in Table 8, of the 24 couples with a high-high pattern of individual psychological health, only six were rated at the highly competent level of marital competence. Another six couples were rated as having dysfunctional marital structures (dominant-submissive, complementary or conflicted). Twelve of 13 couples rated as having competent but pained relationship structures were of the high-high pattern of individual psychological health. The high-low pattern of spouse psychological health was noted to be associated with all types of marital structures and the low-low pattern was only associated with marital structures of lower levels of competence.

When viewed from the perspective of the couples' levels of marital competence, it is instructive to note that highly competent marital structures involved either spouses with a high-high pattern (six of eight) or a high-low pattern (two of eight). Competent but pained marital structures involved a similar pattern with 12 of 13 couples demonstrating the high-high pattern and one couple the high-low pattern. Dominant-submissive complementary marital structures involved five couples with the high-high pattern, two couples with the high-low pattern, and three couples with the low-low pattern. Conflicted marital structures involved one couple with the high-high pattern, three couples with the high-low pattern, and three couples with the low-low pattern.

DISCUSSION

The data point to a significant relationship between the individual psychological health of husbands and wives and the competence ratings of their marriages. Since correlational data cannot inform regarding the direction of causality, the safest assumption is that the effects are reciprocal; individual psychological health facilitates marital competence, and marital competence facilitates individual psychological health.

Although some current theory suggests a stronger relationship between individual psychological health and marital quality for women than for men, our data are inconclusive in this regard. What can be noted is the different pattern for wives and husbands. For wives, more of the measures are significantly correlated. The measures of state anxiety and depression are significantly correlated with marital competence for women and not for men, while locus of control is significantly correlated for men but not for women. A measure of ego development demonstrates the anticipated correlation with marital competence, but achieves statistical significance only for the wives.

There is also support for relationships between marital competence and socioeconomic status, agreement on terminal values, and women's marital satisfaction.

The data reviewed to this point are consistent with the compositional perspective regarding dyadic relationships; that is, a relationship of high competence is of such quality because it is comprised of individuals who are psychologically healthy. A different perspective on this issue can be obtained by considering the data regarding the individual psychological health of both members of the dyad.

When examined as such, these data, although lending some support to the compositional perspective, suggest that other factors play important roles in the determination of relationship competence. Although six of the eight highly competent marriages were comprised of couples with a high-high pattern of individual psychological health, these six couples emerged from a group of 24 couples with the high-high pattern. In other words, 18 of the 24 couples with a high-high pattern did not present with highly competent relationship structures. Indeed, another six couples with a high-high pattern of individual psychological health had clearly dysfunctional marital structures, and 12 couples had competent-but-pained relationships. Despite the small numbers in each subgroup, it appears that couples in which both spouses have average or higher levels of psychological health have an equal likelihood of having either a highly competent or a clearly dysfunctional relationship structure.

Couples with a high-low pattern of individual psychological health had relationship structures that also varied from highly competent to clearly dysfunctional. Couples with a low-low pattern of individual psychological health, however, had only dysfunctional marital structures.

Thus, it appears from these data that although compositional influences on the quality of a relationship do operate, they are but a partial explanation. There are, however, several factors that may have influenced these findings. The first is the small sample size — particularly when the group of 38 couples was divided into subgroups. A second is that the sample was restricted socioeconomically and ethnically. A third factor is that rating an individual's level of psychological health on the basis of 10 psychological measures is but one approach to the assessment of individual psychological health.

From a different perspective, however, there is the possibility that all of our standard measures of psychological health do not emphasize sufficiently the capacity for effective relationships. It may be that the current emphasis on separation-individuation and subsequent autonomous functioning is so pervasive that the capacity for achieving closeness and intimacy has been relatively neglected in our standard measures of psychological health. Some support for this perspective comes from such diverse sources as self-psychology, new developments in conceptualizing the development of the sense of self in women, and early infant research.

Recent reviews of the self-psychology construct of the self-object underscore the continuing need of the individual for another person to regulate self-esteem throughout the life span (Wolf, 1980). Even a relatively autonomous individual has such a need and, although that need may become less intense and more diffuse in adulthood, the need persists. The self-object concept can be understood, in part, as a new emphasis on the role of relationship in psychological health.

A number of students of women's development have recently emphasized that viewing women's development from the perspective of data from the study of men's development, with its emphasis on separation-individuation, does injustice to the central role of relationships in the development of a sense of self in women (Miller, 1984; Kaplan, 1984; Surrey, 1985; Kaplan, Klein, & Gleason, 1985). Although these writers are primarily concerned with the criteria by which women's development is assessed, they also speak to the distortions introduced if men's development is assessed almost solely from the perspective of the separation-individuation metaphor without sufficient attention to the capacity for relationship.

Finally, a variety of studies of the infant fail to support the construct of a normal symbiotic stage from which the infant must separate and individuate (Stern, 1985). These studies reveal that very young infants are exquisitely sensitive to their interpersonal environments and appear capable of at least rudimentary relationships. Thus, the need to consider the development of a relational self in tandem with prevailing emphasis on separation-individuation may not have received sufficient attention, in part because development was understood to start with symbiosis.

These developments are but examples that may suggest that the capacity for relationship has been neglected in our thinking about and measurement of psychological health. If this reasoning has validity, it may explain in part why our measures of the individual psychological health of the spouses appear to explain but a small part of the quality of their relationships.

Although it may never be possible to understand all the factors that, in concert, account for the quality of a dyadic relationship, our data can lend credence to the system concept that the whole is greater than the sum of its parts. With this concept in mind, I turn next to the data that demonstrate how well or poorly the couples' prenatal marital competence scores predict the successful incorporation of a child into the family and whether or not marital structure remains stable or changes across the transition to parenthood.

CHAPTER 6

Stability and Change in Marital Structure

The selection of maintenance or improvement of marital relations as one of the two developmental challenges of the transition to parenthood underscores the theoretical position that the parents' relationship is not just an important family subsystem, but that it provides the family with the basic template for the total system structure. If the parental relationship has the characteristics described as highly competent, there is an increased likelihood that the total family system will also be a highly competent one.

That there are exceptions to this generalization is not to be doubted. Indeed, in our earlier work with families containing adolescents, we found a correlation of $r = .52$ between independent measures of parental marital competence and total family competence (Lewis, Beavers, Gossett, & Phillips, 1976). Although this correlation is strong, one might anticipate an even stronger correlation if the parental relationship were the only determinant of family competence.

In Chapter 2 a selective review of current family theory regarding structural stability and change across life cycle transitions was presented. As emphasized in that chapter, much of current theory is based on observations of families presenting to clinicians with crises around family life cycle transitions. The resulting model of the transitional process stresses the necessity of change in family structure, change that some theorists state is predictable and

An earlier version of this chapter was published in *Family Process, 27*, September, 1988. Reprinted with permission of *Family Process.*

others state is unpredictable. What is missing are systematic empirical data, particularly from a nonclinical sample of families. The one empirical study reviewed, that of Raush and his coworkers, found a remarkable stability in couples' conflict-resolution processes across the transition to parenthood (Raush, Barry, Hertel, & Swain, 1974).

In Chapter 3 a selective review of studies of the transition to parenthood that appear most relevant to this report corroborated the importance of the parents' marital relationship in determining the course of pregnancy and early parenthood.

The major hypothesis was that couples with higher levels of marital competence maintain those levels of competence as they experience parenthood. They may show improvement in marital competence, but do not manifest regressive change in the structure of their marriages unless they experience high levels of stress in addition to those of parenthood itself. Couples with more dysfunctional relationship structures are vulnerable to regressive change in their relationships even in the absence of other types of stress.

A second hypothesis involved the nature of the changes in marital structure. I predicted that when changes occur they will do so in predictable ways. Couples with rigid dominant-submissive, complementary relationships will experience increased conflict and distance. Couples with prenatal relationships characterized by significant conflict will experience increasing disorganization and alienation. In other words, the prediction was that if regressive changes in marital structure occur, they can be described as movement down the *Continuum of Marital Competence* (Lewis, 1986).

Marital Competence ratings were made at Time 1 (prenatally), at Time 3 (three months postpartum) and at Time 4 (one year postpartum). At Time 3, the marital competence ratings were made by the same senior investigator who made the Time 1 ratings. This rater was not blind to his Time 1 ratings when Time 3 ratings were made. In the attempt to assess whether this rater's scores at Time 3 were systematically affected by the experience of scoring marital competence of these couples at Time 1, a second rater, blind to all other data about these couples, scored 10 of the couples at Time 3. Interrater reliability between these two raters was high ($r = .95$, $p < .001$). At Time 4 a second senior investigator blind to all previous marital competence assessments rated the couples' levels of marital competence and his ratings are used in the data analysis. To assess reliability of the Time 4 scores, a second rater also rated 16 of the 38 couples. Their interrater reliability was acceptable ($r = .75$, $p < .01$).

The definition of change in basic marital structure was defined as two or more points on the *Continuum of Marital Competence*. Because this is a conservative measure, analyses were also done defining a one-point difference as change if that difference resulted in a shift to a different type of family structure on the *Continuum of Marital Competence.* Since these analyses did not differ in any essential way, the two-point index of change will be used in presenting the data.

FINDINGS

As can be seen in Table 1, the majority of couples' basic marital structures did not change over the transition to parenthood. A minority manifested a regressive change, assuming a more dysfunctional pattern. A very small number showed an improvement to more competent interactional structures. There was also an indication that the number of couples demonstrating regressive changes increased throughout the first year of parenthood. In only two of the five couples manifesting greater competence at three months was the improvement maintained at one year.

When we looked at how the transition to parenthood affected the marital structure of couples at different levels of marital competence, some interesting trends appeared.

The highly competent group demonstrated, for the most part, the predicted stability in interactional structure. At one year, six of the eight couples retained a structure characterized by shared power, high levels of commitment, high levels of closeness, high levels of individual autonomy, and the presence of psychological intimacy. The two couples whose interactional structure became less competent demonstrated diminished communication, loss of psychological intimacy, and overall an increased interpersonal distance. Their interactional structures assumed the configuration described as competent but pained.

Table 1
The Transition to Parenthood: Change in
Marital Structure* at 3 Months and 1 Year Postpartum

| | *Evaluation Time* | |
	3 Months	1 Year
No Change	24	22
Regression	9	14
Improved	5	2

$n = 38$
*Defined as a change of 2 or more points on the Continuum of Marital Competence.

Two issues need to be emphasized. First, couples who maintained their highly functional relationship described having to "work at it" because of the demands of early parenthood, including much less time for each other, physical fatigue and, in several instances, infants of either difficult temperament or with illness. These couples experienced strain but were able by dint of considerable effort to maintain their relationship at the highly competent prenatal levels. The second issue is that couples rated as 1s or 2s on the *Continuum of Marital Competence* cannot demonstrate improvement on this same index because the scale goes no higher. Despite this, it should be noted that spouses in such marriages described heightened joy, sharing, and excitement due to parenting and due to their infant.

Overall, the capacity of most of the couples rated prenatally as having highly competent relationship structures to maintain their marital structures at such levels during the first year of parenthood is in keeping with a major hypothesis of this study.

The data regarding the competent but pained couples are, however, not in keeping with that hypothesis. As can be seen in Table 2, this type of marital structure appears most vulnerable to regression throughout the first year of parenthood. By the end of the first year, nine of the 13 couples demonstrated clear regression. Changes in marital structure involved increased dissatisfaction (particularly for wives), increased dominance, which was usually a

Table 2
The Transition to Parenthood:
Change in Marital Structure

Marital Structure	n	Nature of Change	Number at 3 Months	Number at 1 Year
Highly Competent	8	No Change	7	6
		Regression	1	2
		Improvement	0	0
Competent but Pained	13	No Change	8	4
		Regression	5	9
		Improvement	0	0
Dominant-Submissive Complementary	10	No Change	6	8
		Regression	3	2
		Improvement	1	0
Conflicted	7	No Change	3	4
		Regression	0	1
		Improvement	4	2

pattern of husband dominance, and increased conflict between the spouses. These relationships appeared clearly dysfunctional by one year after birth, and had assumed the interactional configuration of the marital types we have termed dominant-submissive or conflicted.

The pattern of change among couples rated prenatally with the dominant-submissive complementary type of marital structure was somewhat mixed at three months, but by one year eight of the ten couples again demonstrated a dominant-submissive, complementary pattern. We did not predict such stability for this type of interactional structure. We anticipated that the demands of parenthood, particularly on the wives, would lead to increasing dissatisfaction and conflict. This happened with the two couples who did manifest regression at one year, but in the majority, early parenthood, despite its strain, did not alter their basic interactional structure.

The conflicted group of marriages proved to be the most unpredictable. At three months, four of the seven marital relationships were improved. Improvement was manifested by clearly diminished conflict, greater closeness, and higher levels of satisfaction. Our impression was that the changes reflected the wives' early joy and satisfaction with their newborn children. At one year, two of the four improved relationships had changed, one reverting to the prenatal (dysfunctional) level of marital function and one showing even more intense conflict accompanied by escalating disorganization. The other two relationship structures remained improved at one year. These results were not predicted by our hypotheses.

In order to understand these data, we performed analyses that explored correlates of structural stability, regression, and improvement. One set of analyses explored whether the prenatal ratings of the spouses' individual psychological health might discriminate between marital structural stability and structural change. Grouping couples evidencing either no change or improvement in marital structure and comparing the prenatal psychological health of those spouses with the spouses in relationships which regressed revealed no significant differences. Comparable analyses explored the relation of regression in marital structure to the spouses' perceptions of support from social networks, their perceptions of life stress, and the temperament and gender of the child. All these analyses failed to find any significant correlates of structural change at three months or one year postpartum.

The only significant relationship to emerge from this series of analyses involved length of marriage. Although length of marriage did not correlate with levels of marital competence, marriages manifesting initial regression at Time 3 were of longer duration (mean of 5-6 years) at Time 1 than marriages that did not regress (mean of 2-3 years). The same trend was apparent but not statistically significant for structural change from Time 1 to Time 4.

DISCUSSION

Most couples with high levels of prenatal marital competence maintained their highly competent marital structure through the transition to parenthood. The remainder of the sample did not show the predicted relationship between prenatal marital competence and structural stability or improvement. The competent but pained subgroup, considered as intermediate between the highly competent and clearly dysfunctional groups in our earlier work with families containing adolescents, proved to be most vulnerable to regressive change in marital structure. The complementary dominant-submissive subgroup, understood from our earlier work to be moderately but clearly dysfunctional, demonstrated a surprising stability of marital structure across this transition. The conflicted subgroup, found to be clearly and painfully dysfunctional in our work with families containing adolescents, was most unpredictable. Over one-half of this small group was clearly improved at three months postpartum, and at one year structural stability, improvement, and regression all were seen.

Although a high level of marital competence predicted structural stability across the transition to parenthood, lesser levels of marital competence had more varied consequences. Couples with the same type of marital structures, however, did tend to respond in similar ways to the transition. A number of interpretations are possible.

The first interpretation is that family development is more complex than the hypotheses allowed. The idea that a *Continuum of Marital Competence* developed from empirical data from families with adolescents could be descriptive of families at the stage of the transition to parenthood was an initial premise. As Combrinck-Graham's (1985) model of family development suggests, however, we may have used a *Continuum of Marital Competence* based on findings from a stage of family development (adolescent children) in which individuation and autonomy are primary goals and applied it to a stage (transition to parenthood) in which attachment or cohesion is primary.

It may be useful to examine this interpretation from the perspective of the individual marital types. The highly competent marital structures are characterized by high levels of closeness or cohesion and high levels of autonomy. The presence of high levels of closeness before parenthood may be a factor supporting structural stability during the transition to parenthood in which cohesion is so important. The competent but pained marital structures demonstrate adequate autonomy, but have problems with closeness. The impact of the demands for cohesion, so much a part of the transition to parenthood, may render this type of marital structure particularly vulnerable to regression. The complementary dominant-submissive marital type is most often characterized by greater problems with autonomy than with cohesion. This may help us to understand the stability of this type of marital structure during this particular transition.

The conflicted subtypes have appeared more dysfunctional than the others during a later stage of family development (adolescent children) in which autonomy is paramount, but are the least predictable in our sample during the first year of parenthood. Most often closeness is absent in this marital type and, from Combrinck-Graham's perspective, more regression toward a disorganized system was predicted but not found — at least in this small subgroup and at three months and one year. This subgroup is the only one of the four in which Combrinck-Graham's model is not corroborated.

The failure to find additional correlates of structural regression and stability (with the exception of longer marriages among those marriages that regressed at three months) is perhaps most easily understood as a finding that underscores the importance of the marital relationship structure itself. Although variables such as the spouses' psychological health, perceived stress, and perceived support from social networks may well be important factors in the transition to parenthood, their influence on stability and change in marital structure may be masked by the greater impact of the nature of the basic marital structure on the response to the transition to parenthood. That is, prenatal marital structure is more predictive of postnatal marital structure than are considerations of individual psychological health, stress, and social support. These factors, at least as they occurred in the lives of these couples, appeared not to affect the basic marital structures.

The construct of family epigenesis receives only partial support from these data and cannot be evaluated fully without presenting data regarding the second developmental challenge, incorporation of the child into the family.

The issue of this family transition as a crisis rests on definition. The data presented here, however, are consistent with a crisis perspective for certain types of marital structures (competent but pained and conflicted) and not for others (highly competent and complementary dominant-submissive). The findings presented here lead to a more specific question than that of crisis versus no crisis: "Which types of marital structure undergoing which specific developmental transitions are most apt to manifest crisis?"

Perhaps more than any specific finding, the results presented here emphasize the impact of a previously determined marital or family structure on the experience of a current developmental transition. The data regarding structural stability or change must also be viewed, however, within the context of the second developmental challenge, the incorporation of the child into the family, and it is to these data that we can now turn.

CHAPTER 7

Incorporation of the Child into the Family

Jerry M. Lewis, M.D., Margaret Tresch Owen, Ph.D., and Martha J. Cox, Ph.D.

The psychological incorporation of the child into the family is a central task of early parenthood. The process of the dyad of wife and husband changing to a triad of mother, father, and baby is complex, however, and often is described at only a very global, abstract level. Just what is meant by "psychological incorporation," for example, is seldom defined. If it occurs simply because the baby is born and two have become three, incorporation is accomplished by definition. If, however, as is surely the case, something more is intended, how is incorporation to be defined and measured?

We believe that the incorporation of the child into the family system is a complex, multifaceted process that begins during the early months of the child's life. The essence of this process involves the child's becoming an active participant in the family's enduring patterns of activity and affective exchange. Perhaps the lack of detailed attention to the processes through which the child is incorporated reflects, in part, a psychological model of the infant that emphasizes autism and symbiosis. The former state negates the possibility of interaction by definition, and the latter state negates interaction through the implication that symbiosis involves absence of a clearly defined self and, hence, loss of interactional capacity.

Margaret Tresch Owen, Ph.D., is Director of Developmental Research, Timberlawn Psychiatric Research Foundation, Dallas, Texas. Martha J. Cox, Ph.D., is Director of the Human Development Research and Training Institute, Western Carolina Center, Morganton, North Carolina. An earlier version of this chapter was published in *Family Process, 27,* December, 1988. Reprinted with permission of *Family Process.*

Recent neonatal research demonstrating the surprising perceptual abilities and interactional capacity of the newborn throws doubt on the constructs of autism and symbiosis and increases the need for a more complex model of how the child becomes a member of the family (Stern, 1985). The demonstrated capacity of the children to interact with their surroundings also increases the importance of parents' abilities to involve themselves with their infants.

Parental involvement occurs at both the dyadic level (M-C, F-C) and at the triadic level (M-F-C). Successful incorporation of the child can be inferred if each parent individually establishes effective involvement with the child and the parents together demonstrate effective involvement with the child. By this reasoning, our approach to the measurement of incorporation of the child focuses on certain dimensions of the mother-child relationship, the father-child relationship, and the mother-father-child relationship.

In taking this position, we emphasize that, however crucial the early mother-child relationship is, a family perspective also involves an appropriate focus on the father-child relationship and, importantly, a significant emphasis on the emerging characteristics of the mother-father-child triad. To focus only on the mother-child relationship is inadequate for the appreciation of the complexity of the interpersonal field and its impact on the child's development.

The major focus of this chapter is the relationship of the parents' marital relationship structure to the incorporation of the child into the family. The central hypothesis is that couples who have evolved more competent marital structures prenatally are more likely to incorporate the child successfully into the family.

METHODS

The marital competence ratings made at Times 1, 3, and 4 have been described. The Time 1 ratings made during the second trimester of the pregnancy are the major predictors. Since pregnancy itself may alter marital relationship structure, it would have been preferable to measure marital competence prior to pregnancy. This was not possible in this study, and the impact of pregnancy on marital structure remains potentially confounding.

Incorporation of the child into the family was considered at both three months (Time 3) and one year (Time 4) using dyadic and triadic measures. At three months each spouse's parenting attitudes and skills were appraised. Parenting attitudes were rated from a two-hour, semistructured, individual interview exploring a variety of topics, including the parent's reaction to and involvement with his or her child.

Transcripts of these interviews were scored on scales rating four qualities of parenting adapted from Ainsworth (undated) and Egeland and Farber (1984) (see Appendix 7). These scales measured each parent's investment in the child, delight in the child, sensitivity to the child's needs, and acceptance of the parenting role. The mothers' and fathers' attitudes were scored by four different raters who had no knowledge of the ratings made on the other spouse or any other information about the family. Interrater reliabilities on the 7-, 9-, 5-, and 9-point rating scales ranged from $r = .81$ to $r = .89$.

The parenting attitude scales were highly correlated, and principal component analysis indicated that a single factor could account for 81 percent and 84 percent of the variance in the scales for wives and husbands, respectively. The variable weights derived from this first principal component were, therefore, used in summing the rating scales to produce a composite rating termed "Investment in Parenting."

Parenting skills were rated following observation of each parent's 15-minute, videotaped play session with the child at Time 3. The parent was asked to play with the child for 10 minutes. After 10 minutes, the parent was asked to change the child's diaper, and then play was resumed until a total of 15 minutes had elapsed.

The parent-child videotapes were scored using scales adapted from Ainsworth (undated) and Egeland and Farber (1984). A composite rating of the parent's "Overall Sensitivity" was constructed by summing the scores from four 9-point rating scales (see Appendix 8) measuring the parent's supportiveness, sensitivity, appropriateness of play, and attitude toward play. Two observers, blind to other information about the families, independently rated the videotapes. Interrater reliabilities on these scales were rs of .80, .94, .94, and .88.

A second composite variable of parental skill, "Parental Warmth," was made by summing two scales rated from the videotaped play. These two 5-point scales (see Appendix 8) were designed for the present study and described the parent's level of animation and the positiveness of the parent's affective tone. Interrater reliabilities were $r = 1.00$ and $r = .88$.

When the child was one year of age, the quality of infant-parent attachment was assessed using Ainsworth's Strange Situation Procedure. The Strange Situation videotapes were coded according to the standard scheme specified by Ainsworth and her colleagues (Ainsworth, Blehar, Waters, & Wall, 1978). All strange situations were coded by two independent raters. Independent agreement on the classifications occurred 85 percent of the time. All disagreements were resolved by reviewing the videotape and reaching consensus.

A linear Security of Attachment index was formed from data obtained in coding the videotaped Strange Situation procedure. This index of security of attachment considered the extent to which an infant's behavior deviated from that of the prototypically secure infant, which is customarily given the attachment sub-classification of B3. On the basis of sub-classifications, ratings of avoidance and resistance in the reunions with the parent, and detailed observers' commentaries made of the infant's and parent's behavior in the Strange Situation Procedure, infants were assigned to one of four levels of security: optimally secure, moderately secure, marginally secure, and insecure.

Measurements of triadic interactional functioning were also made when the child was one year of age (Time 4). Mother, father, and child were videotaped together in a 15-minute play session at home with a standardized group of toys. Rating scales were constructed to quantify aspects of the family's affective and activity subsystems (see Appendix 9).

The Activity Scale (see Appendix 9) contained six points measuring the predominant type of patterned activity exhibited by the family. The patterns were: both parents playing jointly with the child; the parents taking turns playing with the child while maintaining verbal contact with each other; the parents taking turns playing with the child but not maintaining contact with each other; and various patterns of parental competition, parental exclusion, and exclusion of the child.

Three affect scales (see Appendix 9) were constructed, each of which contained three points. The Affective Quality Scale measured the level of pleasure involved in the play period; the Affective Intensity Scale measured the level of affect present regardless of its quality; and the Affective Involvement Scale measured the extent to which the predominant affects were shared by the three family members.

A senior investigator rated each of the 38 families. A second rater, blind to all other data about the families, also rated the 38 families. Interrater reliability was acceptable for the Activity Scale ($r = .88$), the Affective Quality Scale ($r = .81$), and the Affective Intensity Scale ($r = .73$). The reliability for the Affective Involvement Scale, although significant ($r = .48$, $p < .01$), was considered inadequate, and this scale was omitted from the analyses.

Another consideration involved the construction of an overall rating of triadic interactive competence. The scores from the Activity Scale and the Affective Quality Scale were combined to form a 3-point Triadic Interactional Competence Scale. The highest level of triadic competence (*1*) indicated a score of *1* or *2* on the Activity Scale and a score of *1* on the Affective Quality Scale. This level of triadic competence reflected couples who either play together pleasurably with their child or take turns while maintaining verbal contact with each other. A triadic competence score of *2*, the intermediate score, involved the same activity scores but an affective quality rating of less than distinctly pleasurable. A triadic competence score of *3*, the lowest level, involved any other pattern of activity and affect.

In order to test the relationship between marital competence and incorporation of the child measures, separate ANOVAs were performed on each measure.
The ANOVAs were 3 (groups of marital competence scores representing the
highly competent, competent but pained, clearly dysfunctional) × 2 (infant
gender) for all measures, except security of attachment in which only two
groups of marital competence scores were used.

FINDINGS

Table 1 demonstrates that the prenatal ratings of marital competence
predict at significant levels the composite measures of the mothers' warmth
and sensitivity (but not investment) at three months. These data demonstrate
that the wives from clearly dysfunctional marriages score lower in these
measures of parenting skills and attitudes than wives from either the highly
competent or competent but pained marital structures. Marital competence
was found to predict mothers' investment in parenting only for girls (see Table
2). With firstborn girls, mothers expressed less investment in parenting when

Table 1

Mean Scores for Mothers' Parenting Skills and Attitudes
at 3 Months by Levels of Marital Competence

T1 Marital Competence	n	Warmth***	Sensitivity*	Investment
Group A: 1, 2	9	9.00	29.44	1.03
B: 3, 4	13	8.67	30.08	−.60
C: 5, 6, 7, 8	16	6.75	24.62	−.23

*$p < .05$
***$p < .001$

Table 2

Mean Scores for Mothers' Investment in Parenthood by
Marital Competence and Infant Gender

T1 Marital Competence Scores			T3 Investment in Parenthood		
	Males	n	Females*		n
Group A: 1, 2	.24	6	1.82		3
B: 3, 4	.54	8	−1.74		5
C: 5, 6, 7, 8	.31	9	.77		7

*$p < .05$

marital relationships were not highly competent than when they were highly competent. If the firstborn was a boy, the nature of the prenatal relationship with the husband did not predict the mother's investment in parenting. These data suggest that for mothers in dysfunctional marriages the gender of their firstborn may be an important aspect of their investment in parenting. It also points to a subgroup of infants who may be vulnerable to problems in development: firstborn girls of mothers in dysfunctional marriages.

Infant gender appears to influence the mothers' warmth and investment in parenting (see Table 3). As a group, mothers of boys were warmer and more highly invested than were mothers of girls.

When we turned to fathers' parenting skills and attitudes, we also found that prenatal measures of marital competence predicted fathers' sensitivity and investment, although not warmth, as indicated in Table 4. There were no significant interactions between marital competence and gender on fathers' parenting measures, but fathers' warmth was significantly greater for boys than for girls (see Table 5).

These analyses suggest that the prenatal level of marital competence is a variable that influences both mothers' and fathers' parenting skills and atti-

Table 3

Mean Scores for Mothers' Parenting Skills and
Attitude by Infant Gender

Infant Gender	n	Warmth*	Sensitivity	Investment*
Males	23	8.39	28.70	.37
Females	15	7.14	25.71	−.23

*$p < .05$

Table 4

Mean Scores for Fathers' Parenting Skills and Attitudes
at 3 Months by Level of Marital Competence

T1 Marital Competence	n	Warmth	Sensitivity**	Investment*
Group A: 1, 2	8	7.75	27.62	1.74
B: 3, 4	13	7.38	26.92	−.03
C: 5, 6, 7, 8	15	6.56	22.07	−.78

*$p < .05$
**$p < .01$

Table 5
Mean Scores for Fathers' Parenting Skills and
Attitudes by Infant Gender

Infant Gender	n	Warmth	Sensitivity	Investment
Males	22	7.59	26.00	.03
Females	15	6.40	23.73	.58

*$p < .05$

Table 6
Mean Scores for Level of Security in Infant-Mother
Attachment by Marital Competence and Infant Gender

T1 Marital Competence Score		Security of Attachment to Mother		
	Males	n	Females	n
1, 2, 3	2.08	12	3.60	5
4, 5, 6, 7, 8	2.40	10	2.30	10

$F = 4.00$, $p < .05$

tudes at three months postpartum. Gender effects are also important, and firstborn girls may be a vulnerable subgroup when their mothers' levels of marital competence are considered.

When the focus was turned to the one-year data regarding infant-parent attachments, the division of levels of marital competence into three groupings (as in the other analyses) did not indicate significant differences in the security of attachment. A division into two levels of marital competence (thereby increasing the power to detect differences due to marital competence) yielded findings that paralleled the three-month data. As shown in Table 6, there was a significant interaction between marital competence and gender. Infant girls of the mothers from highly competent marriages were more apt to be securely attached to their mothers than were infant girls of mothers from more dysfunctional marriages, but there was no effect of prenatal marital competence on the security of infant-mother attachments for boys.

There was a trend for an effect of marital competence on infant-father attachment (see Table 7), with more competent marriages related to more secure infant-father attachments. There were no significant main effects of infant gender or interaction effects on the security of infant-father attachment.

Table 7

Mean Scores for Level of Security in Infant-Father
Attachment by Marital Competence

T1 Marital Competence Score	Attachment to Father (Males and Females)
1, 2, 3	2.9 (16)
4, 5, 6, 7, 8	2.3 (18)

$F = 3.63, p < .07$

Table 8

Mean Scores for Triadic Interactional Competence by
Prenatal Marital Competence

T1 Marital Competence*	n	Triadic Interactional Competence
1, 2	9	1.22
3, 4	11	2.09
5, 6, 7, 8	14	1.71
Lower Scores = More Positive Qualities		

$*F = 4.46, p < .03$

Thus, prenatal marital competence levels tended to predict infant-parent attachment behaviors, and there were infant gender differences in the pattern of effects for mothers.

Table 8 reports the effect of prenatal marital competence on triadic system measures. In this analysis the composite triadic interactional competence scores (activity pattern plus affective quality) were used. Higher levels of prenatal marital competence predicted more competent levels of triadic interaction. Couples rated as having highly competent marriages before their first child was born had higher levels of triadic interactional competence. These data are in keeping with the three-month parenting skills and attitude data and the one-year attachment behavior data.

A question could be raised, however, regarding the degree to which relative marital competence ratings predict incorporation of the child independent of ratings of each parent's psychological health. As noted in Chapter 5, there were modest and significant correlations between the measures of individual psychological health and marital competence at Time 1. In order to explore the possibility that the relations found between marital competence and incorporation of the child measures were merely reflections of relations with individual psychological health, analyses of covariance were performed, testing the effects of prenatal marital competence on measures of incorporation of the child after adjusting for the effects of individual psychological health.

In these analyses, the measure of individual psychological health used was the clinician's overall rating based on the ten psychological tests. These are presented in Tables 9 and 10. Two sets of ANCOVAs were performed. The first used the psychological health of the individual parent as a covariate; the second used the sum of the psychological health scores for both parents as the covariate.

As can be noted in Tables 9 and 10, controlling for the effects of individual psychological health in the form of a covariate in the analyses, either singly (M or F alone) or jointly (M and F together), did not influence the ability of prenatal marital competence to predict these measures of incorporation of the child into the family at three months and one year of age. This finding supports the importance of relational measures in understanding family systems and the development of the child.

In Chapter 4, the ability of measures of marital satisfaction to predict subsequent events was discussed. In this sample of couples, the mean scores for wives' marital satisfaction (MRI) were 106.7 at Time 1 and 101.8 at Time 4 (marital satisfaction unfortunately was not measured at Time 3). The mean scores for husbands' MRI scores were 104.8 and 102.8 for Times 1 and 4 respectively. These modest changes were not statistically significant.

The question of whether marital satisfaction or marital competence at Time 1 is a more effective predictor of family developmental events at one year could be addressed by our data. Neither husbands' nor wives' prenatal marital satisfaction scores predicted regression or stability in the basic marital structure at one year. Wives' marital satisfaction scores were not significantly correlated with any of the measures of incorporation of the child into the family. Husbands' marital satisfaction scores were correlated with both maternal warmth and investment in parenting ($r = .35$, $p < .05$), but not with any of the dyadic measures involving husbands themselves. The husbands' marital satisfaction scores were also correlated with the measure of triadic competence ($r = .37$, $p < .05$).

These few correlations suggested that when husbands were more satisfied with their marriage prenatally, wives were more invested in and warmer with their child, and the family interaction was viewed as more competent when the child was one year. With the exception of these few correlations, however, marital satisfaction was unrelated to other measures of incorporation of the child and was, therefore, not as potent a predictor of subsequent developmental events as marital competence.

Table 9
Transition to Parenthood — Summary of ANOVAs and ANCOVAs

Comparison of significant main effects of prenatal marital competence on measures of incorporation of the child, with and without parental prenatal psychological health covariates.

Incorporation of the Child Measures	ANOVA		ANCOVA, Covariate = Individual Parent's Psychological Health		ANCOVA, Covariate = Sum of Mother's & Father's Psychological Health	
	SS	F	SS	F	SS	F
3 month Parenting						
Mothers: Warmth	39.09	9.96**	39.43	9.66*	40.41	10.30***
Sensitivity	246.19	4.09**	169.09	2.80*	127.47	2.12
Fathers: Warmth	9.05	1.62	4.09	.72	7.92	1.42
Sensitivity	232.16	5.78	191.51	4.66**	225.49	5.62**
Investment	26.07	4.57**	25.77	4.39**	32.24	5.68***
12 Mo. Triadic Interaction Triadic Interactional Competence	3.74	4.32**	N.A.	N.A.	4.93	5.69**
12 Mo. Security of Attachment to Father	3.69	3.58*	4.69	4.68**	3.70	3.59

*$p < .10$
**$p < .05$
***$p < .01$

Table 10
Transition to Parenthood—Summary of
ANOVAs and ANCOVAs

Comparison of significant interactive effects of marital competence and infant gender on measures of incorporation of the child, with and without psychological health covariates.

Incorporation of the Child Measures	ANOVA		ANCOVA, Covariate = Individual Parent's Psychological Health		ANCOVA, Covariate = Sum of Mother's & Father's Psychological Health	
	SS	F	SS	F	SS	F
3 Month Parenting Mother's Investment in Parenthood	18.71	3.66**	18.29	3.75**	19.16	3.75**
12 Month Security of Attachment to Mother	5.41	4.00**	5.28	3.80*	5.16	3.78*

*p < .10
**p < .05

The relationship between the data regarding change in the structure of the marital relationship and the data regarding incorporation of the child was approached in several ways. A series of ANOVAs with marital competence at Times 1, 3, and 4 considered as a repeated measure were done to explore the relationship of changes in marital competence across the three data collection periods to incorporation of the child measures at three months and one year.* These analyses supported the findings regarding the relation between the level of marital competence and incorporation of the child. However, there were no significant interactions to indicate a relationship between the patterning of marital competence over time and measures of incorporation of the child. Thus, no significant relation between regression in marital structure and parenting/child outcomes was found. Couples who experienced regression in their relationship structure were not more likely to have difficulty in the process of incorporating the child than were those whose relationship remained stable or improved.

Finally, the relationship of Time 3 and Time 4 ratings of marital competence to measures of incorporation of the child was explored in a series of analyses of variance.* When couples were in competent marriages at Time 3, mothers were warmer and more sensitive with their three-month-old infants and both parents were more invested in parenting. Higher levels of marital competence at Time 3 also predicted higher levels of triadic interactional competence at one year, but were unrelated to the security of attachment at one year.

Time 4 marital competence ratings were related to security of infant-mother attachment, but not to infant-father attachment. The relation between Time 4 marital competence ratings and triadic interactional competence just missed the .05 level of significance.

In summary, there was but modest evidence for a relationship between two developmental challenges of this stage of the family life cycle. From the standpoint of the measures regarding incorporation of the child, it appears that it is the level of marital competence at a particular time that is important, rather than whether the level of marital competence has remained the same, regressed, or improved.

DISCUSSION

The data presented support the concept that the quality of the parental marriage, as measured prenatally, predicts the incorporation of the child at both three months and one year. At three months the level of prenatal marital

---

*These analyses are available from the authors upon request.

competence influences both parents' relationships with their child, using both interview and systematic observational data. Parents from highly competent marriages are more apt to show greater investment, sensitivity, and warmth in discussing and interacting with their child than are parents from dysfunctional marriages.

The gender of the child also appears to play a role, particularly for mothers and firstborn girls. An interaction was found between mothers' overall investment in parenting, level of prenatal marital competence, and the child's gender. Unless the mother is involved in a highly competent marriage, she invests less vigorously in parenting if her firstborn child is female. This finding and the others reported need replication, both because of the small number involved when our sample is categorized by levels of marital competence and gender of the child, and because, if replicated, the findings point to a group of children who may be vulnerable to developmental problems.

The findings at one year generally confirm the three-month data. Mothers in more competent marriages were more likely to foster their infant daughters' secure attachment than were mothers in less competent marriages. However, differences in marital competence were unrelated to the security of infant boys' attachments to mother. This finding parallels the data regarding mothers' investment at three months, except that the attachment data do not show a reduced likelihood of secure attachment for mothers in less competent marriages, but only increased likelihood of secure attachment in the presence of a highly competent marriage. For fathers there was a trend for marital competence to predict the security of infant-father attachment, regardless of infant gender.

The data from the measures of mother-father-child interaction at one year also demonstrated that levels of prenatal marital competence predict more successful incorporation of the child into the family. Couples with highly competent prenatal marital structures were more likely to demonstrate patterns of activity and affect that suggest successful incorporation when the child is one year old. These analyses were designed to measure early family system characteristics and add weight to the suggestion that the manner in which the couple resolves key issues in the stage of relationship formation forms a basic template for the characteristics of the evolving triadic system. Taken as a whole, the data regarding the incorporation of the child support the construct of epigenesis as it applies to family systems.

CHAPTER 8

Family of Origin

*Jerry M. Lewis, M.D., Margaret Tresch Owen, Ph.D.,
and Martha J. Cox, Ph.D.*

In an earlier report from our research, we reported that selected family of origin variables, marital competence, and individual psychological health all measured prenatally predicted significant amounts of the variance in parenting skills at three months for both mothers and fathers (Cox, Owen, Lewis, Riedel, Scalf-McIver, & Suster, 1985). In general, childhood recollections of both parents were significant predictors for the mothers, but only childhood recollections of their own fathers predicted for fathers.

The present chapter addresses a larger set of our family of origin measures and their relationship to the independent measures of marital competence and psychological health and the various dependent measures of incorporation of the child into the family.

THE FAMILY OF ORIGIN VARIABLES

There were 60 family of origin variables measured at Time 1. These variables addressed five domains: perceptions of current relationship with family of origin, perceptions of family unit during childhood, perceptions of parents' marriage during childhood, perceptions of relationship to mother during childhood, and perceptions of relationship to father during childhood. To reduce the 60 variables to a manageable number, we elected to combine variables that addressed conceptually similar constructs. Both principal component analyses and factor analyses with varimax rotation were used to

Table 1
Family of Origin (F.O.O.) Factors Derived for
Husbands and Wives from Time 1 Variables

1. Current relationship with mother
2. Current relationship with father
3. Cohesiveness of childhood family unit
4. Positive maternal qualities during subject's childhood
5. Lack of maternal intrusiveness during subject's childhood
6. Positive paternal qualities during subject's childhood
7. Lack of paternal intrusiveness during subject's childhood
8. Closeness of parent's relationship during subject's childhood

examine the structure of the variables within each of these domains of family of origin relationships. After meaningful factors were derived by these techniques, subjects were given individual scores based on these factors, and the factor scores were employed in the subsequent analyses.* The resulting eight family of origin composite scores defined the factors shown in Table 1.

As expected, the eight family of origin factors were not independent of each other; rather, there was considerable overlap. Twelve of the 28 intercorrelations among the family of origin factors for wives were significant ($rs = .33$ to .79), and perceptions of parents' relationship and perceptions of the family unit during childhood were most frequently related to the other factors. For husbands, 10 of the 28 intercorrelations were significant ($rs = .33$ to .75) and the perceptions of parents' relationship factor was most frequently correlated with the other family of origin factors.

The correlations between husbands' and wives' perceptions of their families of origin were weak. Fewer correlations than would be expected by chance were significant at the $p < .05$ level. It thus appears that within a marriage, husbands and wives do not tend to report similarly positive or negative views of their families of origin.

FAMILY OF ORIGIN FACTORS, PSYCHOLOGICAL
HEALTH, AND MARITAL COMPETENCE

An issue of theoretical importance is the relationship between family of origin factors and both psychological health and marital quality. Most theories of individual personality development place major emphasis on the

---

*The results of the principal component analyses and the factor analyses and the resulting structure of each of the eight family of origin factors for husbands and wives are omitted for reasons of space and are available from the authors.

rearing environment. Families of origin with open expression of affection, the encouragement of individuality, and other positive characteristics are considered to facilitate psychological health. From such a perspective a strong and positive correlation between family of origin factors and psychological health would be anticipated.

It is also thought, however, that some individuals with less than optimal rearing environments may give positive reports about their families of origin, either as the result of psychological denial, a response bias, or both. To complicate the matter even more, a finding from our research group's earlier, descriptive studies involved adults with high levels of psychological health who reported clearly dysfunctional families of origin (Lewis, Beavers, Gossett, & Phillips, 1976; Lewis & Looney, 1983).

It seems clear that an individual's level of psychological health is determined by a broad array of biological, developmental, and social system variables. Further, we do not know how an individual's level of psychological health influences the recall of family of origin variables. For these reasons, it would be unrealistic to expect an overly strong statistical relationship between measures of psychological health and the subjects' reports of their family of origin experiences.

When the focus is turned to the relationship between family of origin influences and marital quality, the theoretical positions are less compelling. Although a number of theories of mate selection and relationship formation posit that individuals unconsciously select partners with whom early family of origin relationships can be either reenacted or "healed," some of the theories suggest that the family of origin influences on marriage are incorporated within the level of psychological health. Many theories simply do not address the issue.

Since the data regarding family of origin factors, psychological health, and marital competence were derived independently, the analyses exploring their relationships should provide useful insights into these important theoretical issues. The results of two types of analyses will be presented: Pearson correlations and multiple regression analyses.

In Table 2 the significant correlations between family of origin factors and psychological health are shown.*

As can be noted, three of the eight factors for wives and two of the eight factors for husbands correlated significantly with psychological health, and the factors that correlate were different for husbands and wives.

Table 3 presents the significant correlations between the family of origin factors and marital measures. Only the wives' positive perception of paternal

---

*The details of these and subsequent analyses are available from the authors upon request.

Table 2
Significant Correlations Between F.O.O. Factors and
Psychological Health

Family of Origin Factors	Psychological Health[a]
Wives	
Current relationship with mother	.32*
Childhood family unit	.40**
Parents' relationship during subject's childhood	.37**
Husbands	
Maternal qualities during subject's childhood	.33*
Paternal qualities during subject's childhood	.39*

*p < .05
**p < .01
[a] A composite of 10 standardized measures as described in Chapter 4.

Table 3
Significant Correlations Between F.O.O. Factors and
Marital Competence

Wives

Positive paternal qualities, childhood ←——— −.32* ———→ Marital Competence

Childhood family unit ←——————— .38* ——————→ Commitment

Current relations with father ←——— −.43**

Husbands

Lack of paternal intrusiveness ←——— .37* ——————→ Intimacy

Current relations with mother ←——— .37* ——————→ Closeness

Postive maternal qualities, childhood ←——— .34*

*p < .05
**p < .01

qualities during childhood was correlated with the level of marital competence.
As can be noted, the correlation was negative, indicating that the more
positively wives recalled their fathers during childhood, the less competent
the quality of their marriages.

Some interesting and different patterns were noted in the correlations
between the family of origin factors and the variables assessed in arriving at
the marital competence scores. Two of the wives' family of origin factors were

positively correlated with commitment to the marriage, whereas some of the husbands' family of origin factors were positively related to closeness and intimacy in the marriage.

The relationships between family of origin, psychological health, and marriage were next examined using multiple regression techniques. Such techniques were used for two purposes: first, to address the predictive significance of family of origin relationships when either psychological health or marital competence was controlled; and second, to examine the relative predictive value of the various family of origin factors we had defined. We did not make an a priori prediction regarding which family of origin factors or which group of factors would be most predictive of either health or marital competence. We therefore used a stepwise multiple regression analysis procedure to "choose" family of origin factors in the regression analyses after a first step in which either marital competence or psychological health was entered into the equation in order to hold those potential effects constant. These analyses thus provide a way of exploring the relations between the family of origin factors and psychological health after controlling for the influence of marital competence, and similarly the relations between family of origin and marital competence after controlling for the influence of psychological health.

After controlling for effects of marital competence, higher levels of the wives' psychological health were predicted by more positive recollections of their family in childhood ($R^2 = .23$, $F = 10.33$, $p < .01$). For husbands, family of origin factors were no longer predictive of their psychological health after controlling for effects of marital competence. To put this in different terms, a family of origin factor of wives predicted wives' psychological health independently of the quality of their marriages, but the husbands' family of origin factors did not predict the level of the husbands' psychological health independently of the quality of their marriages.

A similar pattern was seen in exploring the ability of family of origin factors to predict levels of marital competence after controlling for the influence of both husbands' and wives' psychological health. Two aspects of wives' relationships with their fathers significantly predicted marital competence after controlling for levels of husbands' and wives' psychological health ($R^2 = .19$, $F = 4.01$, $p < .05$). The relationship was such that positive recollections of father predicted lesser levels of marital competence. As shown in the correlational analyses, husbands' family of origin factors were not significant predictors of marital competence in these multiple regression analyses.

Thus, it appears that family of origin factors operate differently in regard to psychological health and marital competence for the men and women in this study. For wives, both psychological health and marital competence could be predicted from family of origin factors when either psychological health (in the case of predicting marital competence) or marital competence (in the case of psychological health) was held constant. For men, however, the relations demonstrated between family of origin and psychological health in the correlational analyses were not shown in the multiple regression analyses when effects of marital competence on psychological health were first taken into account. The husbands' family of origin factors were not seen to be related to marital competence.

FAMILY OF ORIGIN FACTORS AND STABILITY AND CHANGE IN MARITAL STRUCTURE

It is to be recalled that none of the variables reported in earlier chapters were significantly associated with change in the structure of the marital relationship across the transition to parenthood with the exception of the prenatal marital competence ratings and the length of marriage. More competent marital structures were more likely to remain stable, and less competent marital structures were more likely to regress.

In the effort to explore whether family of origin factors were predictive of change in marital structure, stepwise multiple regression analyses were again performed. In these analyses we attempted to predict Time 4 marital competence from the family of origin factors after first controlling for Time 1 marital competence ratings. The stepwise regression procedure selected wives' childhood recollections of their fathers ($F = 3.58, \ p < .07$) as the only additional predictor. Time 1 marital competence explained 24 percent of the variance in Time 4 marital competence, and the wives' recollections of their fathers accounted for an additional eight percent. Thus, we could account for 32 percent of the variance in Time 4 marital structure, but only eight percent of that variance in the change in marital structure across the transition to parenthood was from family of origin factors.

FAMILY OF ORIGIN FACTORS AND INCORPORATION OF THE CHILD INTO THE FAMILY

As described in Chapter 7, we chose three approaches to the measurement of incorporation of the child into the family. Two of these measures were dyadic (parent-child), and one was triadic (mother-father-child). In this section we explore the relationship between family of origin factors as measured prenatally and the three measures of incorporation of the child. Results from both correlational and multiple regression analyses will be presented.

Parenting at Three Months

At three months we used two measures of parenting: an interview-derived rating of adjustment to parenting and an observationally based rating of parental sensitivity. Table 4 presents the significant results from the correlational analyses with the family of origin factors. As can be noted, one of the husbands' family of origin factors, lack of paternal intrusiveness, was significantly correlated with adjustment to parenting, and there were three significant correlations between two of the wives' family of origin factors and the three-month parenting measures. For wives, lack of maternal intrusiveness was positively correlated with adjustment to parenting and parenting sensitivity, but a positive recollection of paternal qualities during childhood was associated with lesser levels of parenting sensitivity.

Multiple regression analyses were next used in order to address the role of family of origin factors in predicting adjustment to parenthood and parenting skills after controlling for the effects of both psychological health and marital competence.

For wives, two of the family of origin factors, lack of maternal intrusiveness and positive recollections of father, significantly predicted three-month parental adjustment ($R^2 = .26$, $F = 5.82$, $p < .01$) and sensitivity ($R^2 = .28$, $F = 6.47$, $p < .01$) after controlling for effects of psychological health and marital competence. As was found in the correlations, the wives' positive recollections of father predicted a lower degree of observed parenting sensitivity and parental adjustment.

Table 4
Significant Correlations between F.O.O. Factors and
Parenting at Three Months

Husbands

Lack of paternal intrusiveness ←——— .55*** ———→ Adjustment to parenting

Wives

Lack of maternal intrusiveness ←——— .37* ———→ Adjustment to parenting

.43*

Paternal qualities, childhood ←——— −.32* ———→ Parenting sensitivity

---

*p < .05
**p < .01
***p < .001

For husbands, after controlling for the effects of psychological health and marital competence, there was a trend for lack of paternal intrusiveness to predict fathers' adjustment to parenting ($R^2 = .09$, $F = 3.26$, $p < .10$). Given that the husbands' recall of a lack of paternal intrusiveness was highly correlated with adjustment to parenthood before marital competence and psychological health were taken into account, it appears that family of origin does not influence fathers' adjustment to parenthood with much independence from the influences of marriage and psychological health.

In these analyses, family of origin factors were related to parenting at three months, and they operated with greater independence from psychological health and marital competence in wives than they did in husbands. Moreover, these effects for wives were such that positive recollections of fathers (reporting closeness, sensitivity) were predictive of less effective parenting while recalling a lack of intrusiveness from their mothers predicted better parenting.

Security of Attachment at One Year

As can be seen in Table 5, three of the husband's family of origin factors correlated significantly with the security of infant-father attachment and each of the factors involved the husbands' relationships with their own fathers. There were no significant correlations between the wives' family of origin factors and infant-mother attachment when infant sons and daughters were grouped together. Considered separately there was only one significant correlation—for the mothers of daughters. This single correlation is fewer than would be expected by chance, but we will describe it because it corresponds to the unexpected negative correlations found between wives' family of origin factors and their parenting: the more positively these new mothers recalled their own mothers during childhood, the less likely their infant daughters were securely attached to them.

Table 5
Significant Correlations Between F.O.O. Factors and
Security of Attachment at One Year

Husbands	
Current relations with father	$r = .44$**
Lack of paternal intrusiveness during subject's childhood	$r = .41$**
Paternal qualities during subject's childhood	$r = .35$*
Wives	
Maternal qualities during subject's childhood girls, only	$r = -.57$*

*$p < .05$
**$p < .01$

These relations were next addressed using multiple regression techniques in order to control for the influences of marital competence and psychological health, when considering the prediction of infant-parent attachment from family of origin factors.

Similar to the correlational analyses, the multiple regression analyses found that the security of infant-mother attachment was not significantly predicted from the wives' family of origin factors after controlling for effects of psychological health and marital competence. Family of origin effects were found, however, for infant-father attachment. The husbands' reports of positive current relationships with their fathers significantly predicted security of infant-father attachment after controlling for effects of marital competence and psychological health ($R^2 = .17$, $F = 5.74$, $p < .05$). The implications are clear: for wives, these family of origin factors were less influential in predicting the security of attachment than they were in predicting three-month parenting, while there was relatively more evidence for the influence of family of origin on infant-father attachment than there was for infant-mother attachment.

Triadic Competence at One Year

Results from the correlational analyses designed to explore the relationship of the family of origin factors and the overall measure of triadic competence are presented in Tables 6 and 7.

For wives, positive perception of the parental marriage during childhood was negatively correlated with triadic competence — but this was primarily due to the strong effect for daughters, not for sons. For husbands, however, a very different pattern was noted. There were many significant effects. Four of the eight family of origin factors, three of which involved the husbands' relationships with their mothers, were significantly correlated with triadic competence. Two additional factors approach significance in relation to tri-

Table 6
Significant Correlations Between Wives' F.O.O. Factors
and Triadic Competence

	Correlations (r)		
F.O.O. Factors	All Infants	Boys	Girls
Parental marriage, childhood	−.37*	−.08	−.70**

*$p < .05$
**$p < .01$

Table 7
Correlations Between Husbands' F.O.O. Factors
and Triadic Competence

| F.O.O. Factors | Correlations (r) | | |
	All Infants	Boys	Girls
Current relations with mother	.45**	.33	.67*
Current relations with father	.24	.25	.23
Childhood family unit	.54***	.46*	.72**
Maternal qualities, childhood	.39*	.19	.53#.
Paternal qualities, childhood	.32#	.16	.51#
Lack of maternal intrusiveness	−.40*	−.43*	−.33
Lack of paternal intrusiveness	.12	−.25	.05
Parental marriage, childhood	.34#	.31	.44

#$p < .10$
*$p < .05$
**$p < .01$
***$p < .001$

adic competence. There were no significant differences between the correlations found for boys or girls.

In this multiple regression analysis, family of origin factors were highly significant predictors of triadic competence after controlling for the effects of both psychological health and marital competence ($R^2 = .50$, $F = 13.38$, $p < .0001$). The largest predictor was husbands' positive recollections of their father during childhood (partial $R^2 = .41$). The wives' descriptions of their current relationships with their own mothers also contributed significantly to the prediction of triadic competence (partial ($R^2 = .09$). Here the direction of the effect was negative—that is, the more positive the descriptions of the current relationship with mother the less likely that wives would be involved in highly competent triadic interactions.

DISCUSSION

When taken together, these analyses provide documentation of the importance of family of origin factors in family development and suggest that such variables should be included in studies of families undergoing various family transitions. Whether family of origin factors will operate as decisively in other family transitions as they do in the transition to parenthood can be studied empirically. Indeed, to fully interpret the results reported in this chapter, there is need for baseline family of origin data, including such fundamental issues as whether recollections of family of origin remain stable across the adult life span or, as suggested by the "personal narrative" perspective on adult development, such recollections are constantly reworked and rewritten (Cohler & Boxer, 1984).

A surprising finding from these data was the evidence that family of origin variables may operate differently for men and women, an observation that needs intensive study. The data suggest that how one's family of origin is recalled has opposite implications for men and women. We would conclude that a man's positive recollection of family of origin and assessment of current relationships with his parents is positively related to a variety of important outcomes. For women, however, such positive recollections and assessments are more likely to be associated negatively with the quality of marriage and both negatively and positively with a variety of parenting measures, infant-mother attachment, and participation in competent triadic interactions. It may well be that when women describe close relationships with their families of origin they are describing participation in enmeshed relationship systems, which does not bode well for the assumption of parenthood.

Although hardly surprising, the data suggest the importance of young fathers' recollections of and current assessments of their relationships with their own fathers as important determinants of their adjustment to parenting.

The data are also important in suggesting that despite considerable overlap, family of origin influences operate independently of measures of psychological health and marital quality.

In sum, the findings from these analyses document the importance of family of origin factors and suggest the need for a more complex model of the relationship of family of origin factors to psychological health, marital quality, and an important family transition.

PART III

Overview and Implications

CHAPTER 9

Overview of Findings

The findings from this initial phase of our longitudinal family development project illuminate a number of areas of current interest to family clinicians and researchers. As happens in such studies, however, the findings leave some questions unanswered and lead to new questions.

The discussion of the findings will be organized from the perspective of six areas upon which the data reflect, followed by the ways in which the data either confirm or fail to confirm specific hypotheses that guided this stage of the research project. The six areas are:

1. The various marital structures identified in our earlier research with families containing adolescent children.
2. The construct of the *Continuum of Marital Competence.*
3. The issue of stability or change in marital structure across the transition to parenthood.
4. The ability to predict successful incorporation of the firstborn child into the family.
5. The importance of the family of origin.
6. The factors that influence the transition to parenthood stage of family development.

1. MARITAL STRUCTURES

The validity of the various marital structures identified in our earlier research with families containing adolescents is supported in a variety of ways by this research and the work of others summarized in Chapter 3. First, it has been possible to observe the various marital structures identified in previous samples in this sample of younger couples and to categorize reliably the type of marital relationship in each of the 38 couples.

The observation that each of the basic marital structures can be identified or inferred in the work of other investigators, who used very different methodologies, also is considered to add weight to the validity of the structures.

The correlational analyses add to the validity of the various marital structures to the extent that they are theoretically coherent or intuitively appealing. The positive correlations of social class, spouses' agreement on values, and individual psychological health are in this realm. The significant correlation of levels of psychological health and marital structure both support compositional theories of marital structure and suggest that psychological health accounts for only a modest amount of the variance in the quality of a relationship. Unless both spouses have less than average levels of psychological health, there is considerable variability in the type and quality of their relationship. These findings support the basic system premise that the whole is greater than the sum of its parts.

In traditional science, the greatest support for the validity of a construct is found in its predictive ability. From this perspective, the data are considered to support the validity of the marital structures. Prenatal ratings of marital structures significantly predict incorporation of the child into the family, a finding that is considered to both add validity to the marital structures and to be a rare documentation of the epigenetic principle in family development.

The data regarding structural stability or change (discussed below) support the validity of the marital structures, although less robustly than the data regarding incorporation of the child. The support is found in the tendency of each of the various marital structures to have its own type of response to the transition to parenthood. Thus, most highly competent marital structures remain stable, most competent but pained marital structures regress, the majority of complementary dominant-submissive marital structures remain stable, and the conflicted marital structures, as suggested by clinically based theories, are most unpredictable.

The data add particular support to the adaptiveness of the highly competent marital structure. Couples presenting prenatally with this type of marriage are very likely to incorporate successfully their firstborn into the family and maintain the quality of their relationship. This finding lends empirical support to the idea that a relationship characterized by closeness, commitment, intimacy, and shared power along with clear individuality of husband and wife is most adaptive during the transition to parenthood, at least among samples such as ours where the couples share certain demographic features (educated, middle class, white). The finding that this type of marital structure was most characteristic of families containing healthy adolescents in our earlier research with two very different samples of families adds credence to the importance of this particular marital structure (Lewis, Beavers, Gossett, & Phillips, 1976; Lewis & Looney, 1983).

Taken as a whole, the data regarding the various marital structures and their correspondence to marital types described by others is thought to add considerable support to the validity of the various marital structures.

2. THE CONTINUUM OF MARITAL COMPETENCE

The question of how the data inform about the basic marital structures identified in our earlier work is different from the implications of the data for the ordering of these marital structures along the *Continuum of Marital Competence*. The various types of marital structure may, as the data suggest, describe much of the universe of marital relationships without, however, supporting their ordering along a continuum.

It may be recalled that the construct of a continuum as applied to families started with several years of theoretical discussions in the late 1960s and early 1970s led by W. Robert Beavers, then a member of the research team. From these theoretical origins, a *Continuum of Family Competence* was elaborated and the Beavers-Timberlawn Rating Scales were constructed. The scales were then used in our two studies of families containing adolescent children and were found to be most useful. Their validity has been supported by the work of others, most recently by Tienari, Sorri, Lahti, Naarala, Wahlberg, Ronko, Pohjola, and Moring (1985) in the study of the adoptive families of children of both schizophrenic and nonschizophrenic women.

In planning this research project, the decision was made to construct a *Continuum of Marital Competence* based on the marital structures found in the earlier studied families along the *Continuum of Family Competence*. This appears to us to be a logical starting point, but it is not without significant inference—that an ordering of marital types along a continuum supported empirically by the study of families at one stage of development (adolescent children) has utility in the study of younger couples at a much earlier stage of family development (the transition to parenthood).

The data from this study offer only partial support for the validity of the *Continuum of Marital Competence* at this earlier stage of family development. Support is found in the ability of the *Continuum of Marital Competence* to predict significantly the incorporation of the child into the family. The ability of this method of ordering marital structures finds only modest support in the prediction of structural stability or change across this family developmental transition. Two types of marital structures do not "behave" as predicted. The competent but pained marital relationships, associated with a high probability of healthy adolescent children in our earlier studies, are most apt to regress to structures considered to be less competent. The complementary dominant-submissive structures, clearly dysfunctional in our earlier work, showed an unpredicted stability (particularly at one year) during this transition. Since, with few exceptions, structural change means regression to a less competent structure, these two types of marital structures do not respond to this transition as is predicted by the *Continuum of Marital Competence.*

In short, the issue of the validity of the *Continuum of Marital Competence* receives only partial support from its ability to predict the structural consequences of the transition. The validity of the *Continuum* does receive support, however, in the nature of the structural changes observed in the 14 marriages in which change occurred. The changed structure in each instance was in the direction predicted by the *Continuum.*

Thus, the validity of the *Continuum of Marital Competence* finds support both in its capacity to predict incorporation of the child and in the direction of the changes in marital structure when such change occurred. The *Continuum* is not, however, a good predictor of structural change. The most that can be said in this regard is that the level of prenatal marital competence is a predictor of subsequent levels of marital competence after the birth of a child.

Perhaps the most judicious summarizing statement regarding the validity of the *Continuum of Marital Competence* is that it continues to demonstrate promise. Further empirical study may yet demonstrate that a different ordering of marital structures is required for each developmental transition. The one exception may be that highly competent marital structures may work well throughout the life span.

3. CHANGE AND STABILITY IN MARITAL STRUCTURE

The preceding discussion has dealt with the ability of the *Continuum of Marital Competence* to predict changes in marital structure. The data reflect on a number of other issues central to current family theory and clinical practice. The central finding in this regard is that both structural stability and change can be considered normative family developmental processes. Structural change is not a requirement of normal development; indeed, when it occurs during the transition to parenthood it is most apt to be maladaptive. Structural stability is the more frequent finding, but the adaptive consequences depend on the nature of the structure that is preserved. For some couples, structural stability preserves a well-working, competent relationship structure; for others a painful, dysfunctional relationship is maintained. Broad generalizations regarding the adaptive consequences of structural stability or change are far too simple. The crucial aspect of the adaptive consequence of change or stability in marital structure, at least for this particular transition, is the issue of which structure is preserved or changed and the type of structure that results.

The data suggest a tendency for couples with each of the various marital structures to have similar experiences with the transition to parenthood vis-à-vis their marriages. Thus, most highly competent and most complementary, dominant-submissive marital structures were stable during this transition. Most competent but pained marital structures regressed, and the conflicted marital structures were least predictable, with structural stability, regression, and improvement all noted. These findings require replication with a larger sample, but they can be understood as underscoring the importance of the interactional structure of a relationship as a critical variable in determining what occurs during a developmental transition. This interpretation is strengthened by the failure to find other significant predictors of marital changes over the transition such as the level of social support, life stress ratings, or the temperament of the child.

4. THE INCORPORATION OF THE CHILD INTO THE FAMILY

It can be argued that the data regarding this issue are the most important findings of this phase of our research. As both clinical and research evidence mounts supporting the crucial significance of family dysfunction in a variety of outcomes, the demonstration that the nature of a couple's preexisting relationship influences each spouse's ability to parent, the quality of their infant's attachments to each parent, and the nature of their triadic interactions must be strongly emphasized. We are dealing here with the very beginnings of family life, a system of dyadic and triadic interactions that have major significance for the individuals and for society.

The data suggest that, to a very considerable extent, relational processes are crucial variables. Further, it appears that in the complex relation between preexisting marital relationship structure and the measures used to illuminate the incorporation of the child, somewhat different processes are implicated for husbands and wives. Also, family of origin influences play a major and, in some ways, independent role in shaping various outcomes of the transition to parenthood, thereby adding support to transgenerational hypotheses. Finally, infant daughters and sons are influenced differently by the factors that mold this transition.

For both husbands and wives the preexisting quality of their relationship is a decisive influence on their attitudes and sensitivity in parenting, their abilities to promote secure attachments of their infants, and their capacities to evolve effective triadic interactions. The analyses suggest the influences of marital relational structure are independent of the influences of individual spouse's psychological health whether considered singly or jointly. This finding gives additional weight to the system premise that the whole is greater than the sum of its parts.

The data suggest that the gender of the infant is a crucial factor in the outcome of this transition. Infant girls in their relationships with their mothers do not do as well if the mothers are involved in dysfunctional marital relationships, but the same is not true for infant sons. These gender effects are not found in the relation between prenatal marital competence and the measures of the relationships between infants and their fathers. These findings may assist in understanding the increased prevalence of certain psychiatric syndromes such as depression in women later in life. At a more general level, however, they underscore the need to attend the gender of firstborn infants in studies of family development.

Family of origin factors seem to operate decisively during this early phase of family development, and they do so differently for men and women. At a general level, when men reported positive relationships with their families of origin, particularly their fathers, subsequently they were better able to parent effectively and enter into better functioning early triadic family systems. For women, however, the prenatal reporting of close relationships with their families of origin often predicted less effective parenting and participation in less competent early triadic family systems. Since the family of origin measures were obtained before the birth of the child, the most likely direction of effects suggests that for some women positive images of their families of origin reflect a level of continuing involvement that adversely influences some parameters of parenting and family functioning.

The data suggest that perception of the family of origin explains more of the variance in wives' parenting after controlling for effects of psychological health and marital competence than in the husbands' case. However, such is not so for the security of infant-parent attachment in which, after controlling for marital competence and psychological health, infant-father attachment is more clearly predicted from family of origin perceptions than is infant-mother attachment. These findings, although suggesting the need for much additional study, indicate the important role of family of origin factors in shaping the transition to parenthood. These factors operate largely independent of psychological health and marital competence.

Two constructs were selected to measure success in the transition to parenthood. In Chapter 7 the analyses exploring the relationship between these two constructs were summarized. It was assumed that couples undergoing regressive change in their relationship competence would be least likely to demonstrate successful incorporation of their child into the family. Curiously, such was not so: there was no relationship between stability or change in marital structure and incorporation of the child. Rather, the level of marital competence at the time, independent of whether it had changed, predicted incorporation of the child. This suggests that marital competence, whether measured prenatally at three months or at one year, has a relationship to incorporation of the child, and change, per se, is not the important variable.

It is not the process of change that influences incorporation, but rather the structural competence of the relationship itself. In family system terms, some couples undergoing regressive changes in their relationships may be able to contain such crises within the boundaries of their relationships, and, as a consequence, incorporation of the child is associated with the general baseline quality of their marital systems.

5. THE FAMILY OF ORIGIN FINDINGS

Perceptions of the family of origin were predictive of a majority of the measures of the incorporation of the child into the family. The data suggest quite different roles for family of origin factors for men and women. Also, different family of origin factors influence the incorporation of the child into the family, dependent on the gender of the child. Since these findings have been discussed in a preceding section, they will not be repeated here.

Rather, the focus of this section will be on the relationships between the family of origin factors and both psychological health and marital competence. As indicated in Chapter 8, there were a number of significant correlations between various family of origin factors and psychological health. These factors were different for men and women. However, after adjusting for the effects of marital competence, only the wives' recollections of the childhood family unit significantly predicted psychological health. For the men, the significantly correlated family of origin factors did not predict psychological health independently of marital competence.

There was but one significant correlation between family of origin factors and marital competence. For wives, positive childhood recollections of their fathers was negatively correlated with marital competence. None of the husbands' family of origin factors correlated significantly with marital competence. Several of the wives' family of origin factors, however, correlated significantly with ratings of their commitment in the marriages, and husbands' family of origin factors correlated with the levels of rated intimacy and closeness in their marriages. After controlling for the levels of psychological health of these men and women, however, only two of the wives' family of origin factors predicted marital competence. These involved childhood recollections of their fathers and their current relationship with their fathers. These were both negative correlations; the more positively wives described their fathers, the less competent their marriages. None of the men's family of origin factors predicted marital competence after controlling for their levels of psychological health.

These data suggest that for men the effect of family of origin perceptions on psychological health is carried by the competence levels of their marriages, and their effect on marital competence is carried by their levels of psychological health, implying that the husbands' family of origin does not influence marriage independently of levels of psychological health, nor does family of origin influence psychological health independently of marriage. For women, however, family of origin factors predict each outcome independently of the other. In addition, similar to the data regarding family of origin and incorporation of the child, positive family of origin recollections, particularly involving their fathers, predicted less competent marriages.

These findings attest to the importance of family of origin factors in women's levels of psychological health and marital competence and the importance of family of origin factors in the incorporation of the child for both husbands and wives. The finding that different family of origin factors are often significant for men and women is little noted in family system literature and needs emphasis.

6. THE TRANSITION TO PARENTHOOD

In Chapter 3 a selective review of the studies of the transition to parenthood was presented. The focus of those studies is what happens to the marital relationship as a result of parenthood. No studies have been located that focus on the incorporation of the child into the family. Taken as a whole, the studies reviewed suggest that the quality of the prenatal marital relationship is an important determinant of the transition to parenthood. Although most couples experience a decline in marital satisfaction or quality during the first year of parenthood, couples with better relationships prenatally continue to have relatively better relationships postnatally. The studies also suggest that couples with egalitarian relationships have less difficulty with the transition than do couples with dominant-submissive or conflicted relationships.

The study reported here confirms and extends the findings presented in the studies reviewed in Chapter 3. The egalitarian relationships noted in several of the studies are related in many ways to relationship structures we call highly competent, the type of marriage that does well in both of the tasks of the transition to parenthood.

The data presented in this report extend the findings of others by presenting descriptions of various marital structures in greater detail and by suggesting that this particular family transition is accommodated to more or less adaptively by different types of marital structures. We have also shown that family of origin data increase understanding of the transition to parenthood.

Perhaps, our research adds most, however, by extending the focus of this transition to include the construct of incorporation of the child. The interests of the research groups cited were in the identification of those factors that determine the quality of the transition, the impact of parenthood upon marital satisfaction or quality, or the ways in which the wives' psychological health influences the transition and, in turn, is influenced by it. From a family systems' perspective, the transition to parenthood is concerned centrally with both the change from dyad to triad and the impact of the change upon the marital relationship.

The apparent independence of the two selected outcomes of the transition underscores the need to study family developmental transitions from more than one perspective. A favorable outcome from one perspective does not translate automatically to other perspectives. As noted earlier, a possible exception to this generalization may be the marital relationship structure initially identified in our work with families containing adolescents as highly competent. Whether this type of marital structure fares as well in subsequent family developmental transitions as it does in the transition to parenthood is, of course, an empirical question to be answered by the longitudinal data.

THE SPECIFIC HYPOTHESES

At the most general level, the central hypotheses were that prenatal marital competence would predict stability or change in the structure of the postpartum marital relationship and the successful incorporation of the child into the family.

The prediction that higher levels of prenatal marital competence would be associated with greater structural stability was supported only in part by the finding that prenatal marital competence levels significantly predicted the postpartum level of marital competence. Our speculation was that life stress, social support, and the temperament of the child would enter significantly into the findings and they failed to do so; it appears that we still have a great deal to learn about the factors that influence the impact of parenthood upon marital structure. At this point in the understanding of the data, it appears that the preexisting level of marital competence has more to do with the impact of parenthood on marriage than the particular intervening events we have addressed.

The hypothesis involving marital competence and the incorporation of the child was supported. Overall, the greater the level of prenatal marital competence, the greater the likelihood of a successful incorporation of the child into the family. The hypothesis was supported for all three indices of successful incorporation, both dyadic and triadic, and at both three months and one year postpartum. Further, the demonstration that prenatal marital competence continued to significantly predict the incorporation of the child when the psychological health of the spouses was held constant is considered to demonstrate the importance of marital relationship measures in this important family transition. The demonstration that family of origin factors explained an often large amount of the variance after controlling for prenatal marital competence levels and psychological health increases our understanding of the complexity of the transition to parenthood.

We had not predicted that the gender of the firstborn child would be a factor in these effects. The implication that it is particularly mother-daughter relationships that may be at risk when marriages are less healthy is considered an important finding.

Our general hypotheses have, for the most part, predicted this important early family transition successfully. Hypotheses about the specific types of marital structures, however, met with both predicted and unanticipated findings.

The highly competent marital structures traversed the transition to parenthood as hypothesized. Couples with this type of relationship structure, with few exceptions, both maintained the competent relationship structure and successfully incorporated the child into the family. When regression in marital structure occurred, it did so in the anticipated direction of increasing conflict and distance.

The couples with competent but pained marital structures did not experience the transition as predicted, but proved to be the most vulnerable of all types to regressive change in structure. Although they did fairly well as a group in the incorporation of the child, the impact of parenthood upon the structure of the marriage was deleterious. Although the possibility that experiencing parenthood might lead to increasing dissatisfaction and conflict in the marital relationship was noted in Chapter 4, the findings concerning this group do not support the primary hypothesis. The data regarding the nature of change in the structure of the marital relationship do, however, support that hypothesis. When change occurred, it did so in the direction of increasing dominance and submission, increasingly overt and intense conflict, and movement toward a much more distant type of relationship. Interestingly, the prediction that this type of marital structure would be most likely to demonstrate improvement in relationship structure was not supported. For all couples with competent but pained relationships in which change in marital structure occurred, the change was regressive.

The complementary dominant-submissive relationship structures do less well in the incorporation of the child than the highly competent and competent but pained type of marriages. However, they were less likely to manifest structural regression in their marriages than predicted, particularly at the end of the first postpartum year. This unanticipated stability in marital structure during this transition cannot readily be interpreted as the result of traditional gender stereotypes because in many of the couples it was the wife who was the more powerful spouse.

For couples with this type of marital structure who did manifest change, the change was in each case regressive.

The conflicted marital relationship structures proved to be the least effective of the four types in incorporating the child into the family and most unpredictable regarding the impact of parenthood upon marital structure. Some maintained their prenatal structure, others regressed, and a few demonstrated improved functioning and decreased conflict. These findings may illuminate clinically based theories of family development that emphasize the unpredictability of outcome. If the clinicians' experience is with conflicted couples, theories constructed on that experience would naturally emphasize unpredictability.

In Chapter 8, Combrink-Graham's theory was addressed by examining the data on structural stability and change during family transitions. I believe that her theory would define the transition to parenthood as a transition shaped by the family's level of closeness. Our data are consistent with that premise save, perhaps, for the conflicted marital structures.

Taken as a whole, the data from this study are considered to support much of that which we originally hypothesized and, at the same time, to reveal a sufficient number of unanticipated findings to suggest that we have made but a modest beginning in clarifying the complexity of family development.

CHAPTER 10
Implications

The researcher exploring individual, marital, or family competence is confronted by an issue at the level of social process. If the research findings are broadly attended, they may come to be understood as the only way to achieve such competence. The data, in effect, become a social mandate. Even if the researcher has carefully spelled out the values underlying the definition of competence, and the contextual variables that impact decisively on that which is possible for individual, couple, or family to achieve, the data may come to be accepted as universal. Bruner (1986), writing about the study of human development, expressed this concern as follows, " . . . once findings are accepted into the implicit knowledge that constitutes culture, once-scientific theories become as reality-defining, prescriptive, and canonical as the folk-psychological theories they replaced" (p. 135).

Another issue confronting the researcher is that even empirically derived definitions of individual, marital, or family competence may seem undemocratic. In a free society who but the persons involved should define the best way to be? This issue becomes even more complex when children are involved, and evidence accumulates that certain types of parental marital relationships, however satisfactory to the parents, may increase the probability of psychological damage to the child. Whose rights are paramount — the parents' to have whatever type of relationship they desire, or the child's to have an optimal developmental environment? Who is to decide whose rights are paramount?

These types of considerations appear to influence many students of marital and family systems to eschew global definitions of optimal marital and family systems. Even when their data seem to indicate clearly that certain types of interactional structures do work best, one is often confronted by the statement that no one type of marital or family structure is considered more adaptive than others. Each has its strengths and weaknesses. This avoidance of a position thought to suggest élitism, to be value-ridden, and to negate the importance of context is, I believe, associated with a considerable loss. Let me illustrate with what I believe is the importance of a global measure of marital quality such as marital competence.

A growing body of evidence supports the crucial nature of the choice of a spouse and the qualities of the evolving marital relationship. Here I will cite briefly but two sources of such data. The first source is a small group of studies that suggest the role of marital variables in the complex etiologies of major psychiatric syndromes. Because it is often not possible to separate individual personality variables and dyadic relationship structures, the studies taken as a whole can be considered only suggestive.

In the area of the schizophrenias, Sampson, Messinger, and Towne (1964) conclude that such disorders in the women studied developed in the context of severe marital conflict. The conflicts grew out of dysfunctional marital structures that, in themselves, were either extensions of or reactions to very disturbed family of origin relationships. Rogler's and Hollingshead's (1965) intensive three-generational study of 20 poor, young schizophrenic men and women in San Juan also documents the complex relationship of marital factors and severe individual psychopathology. In contrast to a carefully selected control group, dysfunctional marital relationships were both a part of the context in which schizophrenia developed and were intensified by the illness.

Evidence also suggests a relationship between marital variables and major depressive syndromes. Examples include the demonstration that the absence of a close, confiding heterosexual relationship is a risk factor for depression for both women and men (Brown & Harris, 1978; Roy, 1981). Weissman (1980) and Rounsaville and colleagues (1979) have documented the often critical role of marital conflict in the development of depression in women and the role of such conflicts as predictors of relapse.

Hafner (1986) has recently reviewed the literature regarding the role of male-dominated marital structures in a variety of severe psychiatric syndromes, and concludes that the evidence suggests that such structures often play a decisive role.

The second source of evidence regarding the importance of identifying and studying both competent and dysfunctional marital structures is a handful of developmental studies that suggest the importance of mate selection and relationship structure in perpetuating or altering developmental trajectories.

Belsky and Pensky (in press) provide a comprehensive review of these studies, and I discuss only two of them here.

Elder and his colleagues, using data from the Oakland-Berkeley Longitudinal Project, report a four-generation process involving deprived early developmental circumstances, selection of an unstable spouse, the formation of a dysfunctional marital relationship, ineffective parenting with subsequent deprivation of the children, and the continuance of the cycle into the next generation (Elder, Caspi, & Downey, 1986). Rutter and his colleagues report, however, that a subgroup of developmentally deprived girls marry stable men, construct harmonious relationships, parent effectively, and, thus, break the anticipated developmental trajectory (Quinton, Rutter, & Liddle, 1984; Rutter & Quinton, 1984; Quinton & Rutter, 1985). In these studies it seems clear that mate selection and relationship formation can be crucial turning points in furthering or interrupting a destructive transgenerational process.

These developmental studies are not without methodologic problems. The complex relationship between personality structures and relationship structures are, for the most part, insufficiently discriminated. Newer methodologies for the study of relationship structure had not been developed and, for the most part, self-report measures are the sole index of relationship competence. Nevertheless, these studies, along with the cited examples of studies suggesting a relationship between marital factors and the development of individual psychiatric syndromes, are, I believe, a strong mandate for the scientific study of overall marital competence, the clarification of various marital structures, and the adaptive consequences of those structures.

Of particular importance is the need to focus newer methodologies on the marital relationship structures that facilitate the accomplishment of both individual and family developmental transitions throughout the life cycle. It is axiomatic that in pursuing such goals the researcher must both articulate clearly the values underlying definitions of competence and dysfunction and clarify the contextual factors that mold and shape the adaptive nature of such types of relationship structures.

In short, I believe that the researcher must do all that he or she can to reduce the likelihood that findings will be interpreted as universal and a canonical process induced. As the research reported in this volume clearly indicates, however, I do not believe that these concerns should cause the researcher to shrink from the task of studying these important relationship issues.

Thus we have discussed the issue of whether or not one should, in view of possible "negative" social consequences, do research exploring relationship competence. A second global issue is whether it is appropriate to use traditional scientific approaches in the study of human relationships. It is not too long ago that I would have considered that question with considerable astonishment. Although my affirmative answer to that question is present on each of the preceding pages, it may be useful to describe the barebones outline of my understanding of the controversy from which the question springs.

For some, the question of the applicability of traditional science for the study of human relationships appears to be based on the philosophy of constructivism. Constructivism denies either the presence or the possibility of proving the presence of a real "out there" world. Rather, reality is a construction of the observer and is validated by consensus. Although historically constructivism can be traced to Kant, I have been instructed in particular by the modern writings of Bruner (1986), Watzlawick (1984), von Glasserfeld (1984), von Foerster (1984), Goodman (1984), and Spence (1982).

As but an example, Bruner (1986) suggests that there are two basic cognitive models, the logico-scientific and the narrative. The former finds its primary use in defining the reality of nature, and the latter in structuring the reality of human affairs. The inability of logico-scientific paradigms to understand human affairs is stated most succinctly by Watzlawick (1984) who divides reality into two parts: "first-order" reality, that of objects, and "second-order" reality, that of meaning, significance, and values. Watzlawick writes, "Relationships are not aspects of first-order reality, whose true nature can be determined scientifically; instead, they are pure constructs of the partners in the relationship and as such they resist all objective verification" (p. 238).

It is, then, from the philosophic tradition of constructivism that questions emerge about the applicability of traditional science for the study of relationship systems. Our answer to such questions is, of course, obvious. Although there are clear difficulties to be surmounted, scientific methods can be productively applied to the study of human relationships. There is a palpable reality to relationship structure; that reality can be rigorously studied using traditional scientific processes. Our research group has done so; the value of the enterprise is ultimately judged by the reader. The project itself, however, is a clear statement of the belief in the usefulness of the scientific study of human relationships.

IMPLICATIONS FOR DEVELOPMENTAL RESEARCH

Perhaps as much as any specific finding, the research data from this project illustrate the impossibility of understanding human development without careful attention to the context. If, for example, a child's development is viewed independently from the nature of his or her parents' relationship with each other, a significant source of understanding will be lost from view. It is not enough to study the child interacting with the mother and with the father.

Although these are important family subsystems, the parental relationship subsystem may be even more decisive in establishing the developmental ambiance for the child. The data from this project suggest that a deeper and richer understanding of the child's development will result from studying the total family system (M-F-C), the parental subsystem (M-F), and both parent-child subsystems (M-C, F-C).

Perhaps an even richer perspective of the child's development can be obtained by the concomitant study of both sets of grandparents, as suggested by some current family theories. It was not possible for us to study directly the grandparents in this research project, and our reliance is on data reported by the parents.

The transgenerational data were collected before the birth of the child and the findings suggest the need to include such data in developing a more comprehensive model of the child's development. In a number of analyses, family of origin factors explained substantial amounts of variance after controlling for levels of parental psychological health and marital competence. The parents' views of their past and current relationships with their own parents appear important to the nature of their child's developmental experiences.

Another finding involves the basic family system premise that individuals within a system impact on the nature of that system's functioning. The impact of the child's gender clearly merits continued study as an important contributing factor to the patterning of interactions within the family system.

The data from this study also have implications for the study of adult development. Almost routinely, students of adult development rely on self-report instruments only to evaluate the individual's interpersonal context. In some instances, such instruments may be only a question or two that can hardly be considered as tapping into the powerful ways in which such contexts can influence an adult developmental trajectory. For example, the assumption of the parenting role is a powerful organizer of adult development. Our data indicating that the quality of a person's marital relationship influences his or her experience as a parent suggest one pathway through which adult development can be influenced by relationship variables.

To move from these examples of the implications of our data for developmental research to the implications of a family systems approach for the study of development, we refer the reader to a recent and thoughtful review by P. Minuchin (1985). She suggests that two factors have hindered the use of family system paradigms by developmental researchers. One is the legitimate methodologic difficulties involved in moving beyond the individual and the dyad, and the second is the tendency to protect prevailing scientific paradigms. It is my hope that the findings presented here can be seen as an example of the rich payoff that can occur for the student of individual development when the individual's family context is studied as a crucial part of that development.

IMPLICATIONS FOR CLINICAL PRACTICE

In this section the implications of the findings will be discussed briefly as they apply to clinical practice in its broad and most general terms. The more focused implications for family theory and therapy will be described in the next section.

Persons seeking help from professionals are usually seen individually, regardless of the nature of their distress. Even when they present to clinicians with concern and distress about their marriages and families, they may be treated as individuals. The major treatment paradigms continue to be individually based, and many professionals are not trained to intervene effectively and comfortably at multiple levels, e.g., the individual and his or her central dyad, or the family. Other professionals with circumscribed training in marital and family therapy do not see individuals, some because their paradigms preclude it and others because of insufficient training. Although the number of professionals who are trained to use multiple system interventions may be increasing, as a group we may still be at what Havens (1973) described as the "mad surgeon" stage. A mad surgeon takes out every patient's gallbladder regardless of what's wrong because that is the one procedure he or she knows how to do well.

The data from this project call for therapeutic pluralism. Marital competence, for example, is clearly a relational construct. It is not the simple addition of two persons' personalities. It is more than the sum of its parts. This point is demonstrated by the finding that two persons with average or greater levels of psychological health may evolve relationship structures that range from highly competent to severely conflicted. As a relational measure, marital competence is a robust predictor of future events in the life of the couple and family, and it operates with considerable independence from certain individual characteristics of the spouses.

This suggests that relational intervention techniques such as marital and family therapies are the measures most suited to intervene successfully in relationship disturbances. Often, the participants in the relationship are able to function as effectively as individuals outside the context of the relationship.

In a similar way, the data on triadic competence suggest that the child is quickly caught up in the parents' relationship problems. Although our focus was not on the child's role in those difficulties (other than the child's gender), it may be anticipated that, if not presently, within a few years the child will be making an active contribution to the family dysfunction. The message for the clinician is training and effectiveness with multiple level intervention techniques.

At a general level, findings such as those presented here argue for the clinician's continual monitoring of the state/trait dialectic. In these days of biological determinism and psychoanalytic renewal, it is often too easy for the clinician to conclude that the patients' difficulties are clearly trait, and lose the often remarkable ability to intervene in that which may be much more a direct reflection of the state of the patient's relationship context.

IMPLICATIONS FOR FAMILY THEORY
AND THERAPY

Family Theory

The implications of these findings for family theory are dependent upon the reader's view of the relationship of research data to theory building. The research reported in this volume clearly follows the traditional scientific approach to research. Several of the findings can be interpreted to refute aspects of some current models of family developmental theory. The implications of our findings for theory, however, are presented without attempting to relate the findings to specific family developmental theories.

At the most abstract level, the data provide empirical support for the basic systems construct that the whole is greater than the sum of its parts. Marital competence is more than the sum of the spouses' psychological health, and is a robust predictor of subsequent events in the life of the family, independently of the spouses' psychological health.

The data also support the importance of interactional structure as a major determinant of what happens during a developmental transition. This issue, little attended to in many family theories, was highlighted originally by Hill (1949) in his ABCX Model and more recently by McCubbin and Patterson (1983) with their revised Double ABCX Model.

The data also support the validity of overall measures of marital quality. Many family theorists eschew overall measures of relationship competence, preferring instead to focus on the strength and liabilities of different types of relationships. The data from our study, particularly the predictive capacity of overall measures, suggest that the issue is far from settled, at least on empirical grounds.

In regard more specifically to family developmental theory and the issues of structural stability or change during transitions and epigenesis, our data support the need for more complex models of family transitions. Such models need to attend the adaptive consequences of structural stability, change to a more adaptive structure, and change to a less adaptive structure, rather than emphasizing solely the positive adaptive consequences of change through crisis. Crisis and positive change to a more adaptive structure occurred in only a minority of our sample; stability in structure was the rule, and when change occurred it was more likely to involve transformation to a less adaptive structure.

It is important to point out that in this nonclinical sample of couples, patienthood did not develop in structurally stable ("stuck") relationships. The increases in the wives' levels of state anxiety, although statistically significant, do not appear to be in the range of clinical syndromes and when present were associated with structural change of a regressive nature rather than structural stability.

The concept of epigenesis as it applies to family development receives empirical support in our data. Couples who present prenatally with highly competent relationship structures were more likely to accomplish successfully the two developmental challenges of the transition to parenthood. Those data may be interpreted as linking together the resolution of one stage of family development (relationship formation) with the successful accomplishment of a subsequent stage of family development (the transition to parenthood).

The triadic competence data may also provide a window through which to study the very beginnings of that which Haley (1981) called perverse triangles. By the time children are one year of age, it is possible to detect parent-child alliances that exclude the other parent and triadic systems that involve intense parental competition for an alliance with the child. If these early structural alignments remain unchanged, we may be observing the birth of dysfunctional family systems that present to the clinician often when the child is at the age of accelerated separation from the family.

The data from this study also illuminate the importance of family of origin influences on family development. Family of origin data collected prenatally appear to be good predictors of many subsequent family developmental processes. These data must be linked to other crucial systems of variables, however, in more complex models than is usually the case. The finding, for example, that different family of origin factors appear to operate, often in very different ways, for men and women has, to my knowledge, received little, if any, previous attention.

Family Therapy

The implications of the data presented in this volume for family therapy depend to a considerable extent on one's perspective on the relationship between theory and therapy. If an individual is never without a set of underlying assumptions about self, the world, and the relationship between the two, then it seems clear that clinical interventions must emanate from some type of explanatory model. The clinician's model needs to be explicit in order to avoid totally personal and idiosyncratic processing of clinical data. Currently, models that attend a wide range of variables at different levels of organization over time such as Engel's (1980) biopsychosocial model are to be valued because they address such complexity.

Haley (1980) suggests a differentiation of research models and therapy models. He emphasizes that research is basically concerned with the "truth"; the researcher strives for objectivity and distance from the data and is interested in all the variables that influence a given situation. In contrast, the therapist is involved in a closer relationship with the data and is primarily interested in simpler ideas that influence people to change. Haley outlines six criteria for a useful theory of therapy. The theory should: 1) be relevant for successful outcome, 2) be simple enough for the "average" therapist to understand, 3) be "reasonably comprehensive," 4) guide the therapist to action rather than reflection, 5) generate hope for therapist, client, and family, and 6) define and explain failure.

These are eminently sensible constructs and I would supplement them only slightly. First, it seems important that therapy models make explicit what is considered "normal," highly adaptive, or what is sought in a successful outcome. Not to make the criteria of successful outcome explicit may either allow the therapist's overt or covert assumptions and values to play a decisive role in such a definition or allow the family to define the outcome. Although the latter course sounds happily democratic, it may not attend the needs of, for example, the symptomatic child whose parents have a sadomasochistic relationship they do not wish to change. The need to make explicit the goals of successful therapy—at least in the mind of the therapist—does not mean disregarding the family's hopes and desired outcomes; indeed, they must be dealt with directly.

A second addition to Haley's list is that a therapy model should not contradict research findings. Haley's work with families containing late adolescent or young adult children suggests that significant structural change of the family system is necessary to facilitate separation of the children. Change is considered a normative, adaptive process at that stage of family development. The data presented here indicate that change as normative process should not be generalized to other family transitions, for during the transition to parenthood change is, for most couples, in the short run, maladaptive.

The family therapist has three basic approaches to the use of theory in therapy. One involves the use of the same theoretical model in all clinical situations. Such a model must be comprehensive in order to deal with the range of clinical phenomena. A second approach, called "pluralism" by Havens (1973), involves using different models to approach different clinical situations as, for example, a behavioral model with one family and a structural model with a different family. This approach taxes the knowledge and ingenuity of many therapists: it is difficult to master techniques derived from a number of very different models. Finally, many therapists operate from an eclectic model in which bits and pieces of several models are combined in an often highly personal way. Although this type of eclecticism is not often lauded, it may be more common than acknowledged.

These and other factors influence the use of research data by a therapist. Many, perhaps even most, therapists may be relatively impervious to such data; some incorporate new findings into the theoretical models that govern therapeutic interventions. Hence, I will select only several of the research findings and suggest their implications for some forms of family therapy.

First, the study of this family developmental transition suggests that the processes involved are more complex than many clinically-based theories suggest. Structural change cannot be unequivocally viewed as positive, and structural stability is not always a reflection of the pathologically "stuck" family. Rather, families may traverse a developmental transition without basic structural change, with change to a less adaptive level, or with change to a more adaptive level.

This suggests that family therapists must both assess current interactional structure and find ways to appraise former structural features if there is the suggestion that change has occurred. This translates into careful assessment. Perhaps the clinical guideline is the greater the complexity, the more extensive the assessment. From a perspective of all transitions in families being pretty much the same to the much more specific perspective that different developmental transitions may be very different experiences for different types of family systems is a giant leap in complexity, but careful assessment of each family leads to the possibility of treatment based on the developmental specifics for a particular family.

The data also suggest that the relationship of family transitions to the development of symptomatic states in family members may be different at different transitions. It is not possible to generalize from "leaving home" to other transitions. It appears that a family member's symptoms may reflect a family context of either structural stability or change, depending on the stage of family life, the structural pattern of the family, and the nature of the change in structure, if such occurs. Once again, research suggests greater complexity and the need for more comprehensive models, thorough assessments, and interventions designed to fit a particular family's specific circumstances.

A second implication of the research data is the suggestion that the repetitive interaction patterns understood at the most abstract level as regulators of distance between the couple and within the family may have clinical utility.

The highly competent, competent but pained, complementary dominant-submissive, conflicted, and severely dysfunctional patterns are clearly structural configurations of a global type.

Most configurations have several subtypes and, in addition, there are crossover types at each interface. The arrangement of these types on a continuum was found to order this sample in a manner that had strong predictive ability. These findings suggest that clinicians may well start their assessment procedures by identifying a couple's or family's basic structural configuration. Although it will be necessary to know much more about each clinical situation, understanding the basic family structure offers a tentative framework from which further explorations may proceed.

The finding that when structural change occurs it does so in a predictable direction may also have clinical utility. It suggests that certain structural realignments may be anticipated. These realignments may be part of an escalating conflict with increasing alienation or a movement from disorganization and chaos toward more clearly defined structure. The clinician may come to recognize the impossibility of facilitating a family's structural change directly from disorganization to flexibility without an intervening phase of more rigid structure.

Although a great deal of work must be done before a broadly acceptable typology of marital and family structures is in place, our research suggests that it may be possible to move toward an empirically-based typology that provides useful, if macroscopic, clinical guidelines.

A third implication involves the findings regarding families of origin. The predictive strength of these data suggests that comprehensive models of marital and family systems need to attend family of origin influences. Although there is much acceptance of the importance of transgenerational influences, the data from this project add needed empirical support. As indicated earlier, however, family of origin factors appear to operate in more complex ways than are often ascribed. For clinicians, two sets of findings need emphasis. The first is that family of origin factors may operate independently of psychological health and marital quality. The second finding is that family of origin factors appear to function differently for men and women.

These findings suggest again the need for more complex models of family development. For the clinician this translates into more thorough assessment procedures and the development of treatment plans that fit the particular family of origin data for a specific family. Gender differences need to be kept in mind.

At a general level, the research data presented in this volume support considerable heterogeneity in family development. A simple clinical formula applied to all couples and families will almost certainly distort the experience of many. The need to move away from such simple formulae to more complex models offers the clinician a considerable challenge. One aspect of the challenge is the mandate to consider each family's particular developmental course. Although our data suggest a small number of courses rather than a random walk, the evaluation of where each family is and where the family has been involves a much more complex task than some theoretical models dictate. While it may be easier to err on the side of oversimplicity, in doing so the clinician may force the family's experience into patterns that don't fit them well.

IMPLICATIONS FOR THE TRANSITION
TO PARENTHOOD

The focus of the studies presented earlier (Chapter 3) was, for the most part, somewhat different from our own. A central finding of those studies was that marital relationship variables are important determinants of the transition to parenthood. A second finding of importance to the hypotheses and data reported here was that although the transition is stressful for all or most couples, couples with relationships rated as stronger prenatally maintained that relative ranking postnatally.

We have confirmed and, I believe, extended those findings. Couples with highly competent relationship structures accomplished successfully the two developmental challenges of this transition. In addition we present data that suggest that certain marital relationship structures may be selectively vulnerable to regression during the assumption of parenthood.

We have added the dimension of the incorporation of the child into the family as a central developmental challenge of the transition. This issue has been little attended by other researchers, and attempts to operationalize and measure it are thought to be significant additions to the study of this family transition.

The finding that there was not a clear relationship between changes occurring in the couple's relationship and successful incorporation of the child into the family emphasizes the need to study different aspects of the transition concomitantly. Studying only one aspect of the transition, such as either changes in the marital relationship or the incorporation of the child into the family, may produce an overly simple view of a complex transition.

In Worthington and Buston's (1986) review of the marital relationship and the transition to parenthood, they developed a theoretical model of the transition. It may be instructive to examine this model from the perspective of our own findings.

The model emphasizes three central constructs that can be easily related to our findings regarding marital competence and the *Continuum of Marital Competence*. The three constructs concern: time schedule disruptions, conflict over relationship rules, and the functioning of the couple prior to the transition.

The functioning of couples prior to the transition can be understood, at a general level, as a way of categorizing couples relationships on the basis of their competence. Conflict over relationship rules relates directly to the role of power in determining marital competence. Time schedule disruption, at first glance a construct of a more circumscribed order, is discussed by the authors from the perspective of its impact on the couple's balance of intimacy and distance. Inasmuch as establishing the balance of closeness and separateness is a central task of early relationship formation out of which the interactional structures that constitute various levels of marital competence are crystallized, the disruption of schedules also relates to the constructs of marital competence and the *Continuum of Marital Competence*.

In a second article, Worthington (1987) elaborates a more general model of family developmental transitions and the matching of treatment interventions to three critical variables. In this later paper, the three critical variables are, in part, different. One is the disruption of time schedules; the second is the number of new decisions involving initial disagreement; and, third, the level of pretransition conflict. Although the latter two variables are stated differently than in the earlier paper, they both relate to the construct of conflict and appear, therefore, to relate directly to the concept of marital competence.

A central question Worthington asks is why some families experience crisis and others do not when faced by the same normative life transition. By using a matrix involving the three variables, he hypothesizes that families with low levels of pretransition conflict, few changes in their schedules, and a low number of initial disagreements are apt to be little affected by a transition. These characteristics are often associated with high levels of marital competence. Although Worthington's model places conflict and, in a different language, power in central organizing roles, there are obvious parallels with the *Continuum of Marital Competence*.

IMPLICATIONS FOR SOCIAL POLICY

The most urgent message for social planning involves the observation that young, educated, relatively affluent couples with little external life stress experienced considerable stress as they assumed the roles of parents. More than one-third of them experienced destructive changes in the basic fabric of their relationships with each other. A sizable number of the couples were demonstrating interaction patterns with their children that appear to be possible precursors to dysfunctional families and symptomatic family members.

This observation suggests that we, as a nation, are doing something wrong: We are not adequately preparing young people for their roles as parents. Collectively we need to rethink the utilization of our educational resources.

If these findings speak to the toll among the more fortunate, what must this transition be like for the very poor, for the disabled, and, most of all, for the single mother who is so often poor and disabled? How devastating must the early experience of parenthood be under such circumstances?

Such social policy issues are made even more urgent by transgenerational longitudinal studies. If one hopes to break the cycle of childhood deprivation, psychological disturbance, conflicted marriage, poor parenting, childhood deprivation, psychological disturbance, and on and on, one point of social action is intervention during the earliest stages of the transition to parenthood.

A second social planning issue involves the need to include education for marriage. The data from this project along with the other studies reviewed indicate that the structure of the marital relationship established early in the marriage is a crucial variable in that which follows—crucial to the spouses, and also crucial for their children. As we accumulate the knowledge, certain types of social interventions should be considered, interventions that hold some promise for the interruption of destructive transgenerational developmental processes and increase the likelihood that families can more readily be nurturing, affectionate, and facilitating social systems.

In a provocative essay, the epidemiologist Leonard Sagan (1988) reviews the factors influential in the dramatic 25-year increase in life expectancy during this century. He concludes that advances in modern medicine, however important for the health of individuals, do not explain the overall health of large populations. This conclusion follows his review of the impact of factors usually considered decisive. Sagan emphasizes that sanitation, augmented nutrition, antibiotics, immunization, and modern surgical approaches to cardiovascular diseases and cancer cannot, in concert, explain the population's lengthened life span.

Sagan suggests that a critical, if little attended, factor is the change in family life, particularly the trend toward smaller families. Family size, he declares, is an excellent predictor of childhood survival. Young children of large families have a higher overall mortality rate than the children of small families, regardless of social class. Sagan believes that smaller family size protects children by the extra nurture they receive from their parents. He states: " . . . whatever the connection, the fact stands that the affection and security associated with the modern family are the best available predictors of good

health" (p. 28). Children who receive such nurturing are better survivors—
they are bigger, brighter, more resistant, more resilient, and they live longer.

However controversial, Sagan offers an intriguing paradigm with which to
emphasize the importance of the family. Although he speaks to population
statistics—trends involved in large groups—he implies something about the
viability of families—yours and mine—over generations. An interesting, if
provocatively self-serving, reason to support family developmental research.

PART IV

Appendices

APPENDIX 1a.

Time 1:
Individual Interview (Prenatal)

1. Vocational

Tell me about your work (what you do, what it's like, how long you've been doing it, how you chose it, etc.)

What are its pleasures? *(instrumental vs. interpersonal)*

What are its problems? *(instrumental vs. interpersonal)*

Will you continue after the baby is born?

How does it fit in with where you see your life going?

Ten years from now; 20 years from now?

Do you feel committed to a career?

What have your "inner dreams" been, about what you want to do?

How much do you get to work on your own and how much direct supervision do you get? Do you like the balance of independence and supervision?

How does your work "mix" with your marriage and personal life?

(For homemaking spouses ask all of the above plus the following:)

If you worked outside the home before, how does working in the home compare?

What, if any, plans do you have about working after the baby comes? How do you see parenting fitting in with your work life?

Do you feel that your homemaking is appreciated by your spouse?

2. Leisure Activities

What do you do with your nonworking hours? (How many of these activities do you do individually? How many are done as a couple?)

Are there particular friends that you enjoy spending leisure time with? What is your relationship with them like? *(closeness, supportiveness)* Do you see these people individually or as a couple?

Are there leisure activities that you'd like to do more of that you aren't able to pursue? If so, why?

3. Marital Relationship

Out of all the people in the world, how did you happen to choose your husband (wife)?

Tell me about your marriage (how would you describe it?)

What do you see as its strengths?

What do you see as its weaknesses?

How close do you feel you and your husband (wife) are?

   Tell me about what makes your marriage close.

Some couples talk with each other about ideas, happenings, etc. Do you and your husband (wife) do a lot of this?

Some couples talk with each other about their everyday feelings—hurts, anger, things like that. Do you and your husband (wife) do a lot of this?

Some couples talk with each other about very private feelings, thoughts, hopes, fears. Do you and your husband (wife) do a lot of this?

How do you and your husband (wife) make decisions?

What about big decisions—like a new car, a job change, whether to have a baby?

What about little decisions—like which movie to see or where to eat?

If you and your husband (wife) really disagree about something, how do you settle it? (A big decision? A little decision? Have there been any? Can you remember the last one?)

Overall, who do you think has the most to say about your future together?

Are you and your husband (wife) openly affectionate with each other?

   Tell me about your sexual relationship.

On the average, how frequently do you make love? Does that satisfy you? Has there been any recent change in the frequency?

How satisfactory is yours and your husband's (wife's) sexual intercourse? (How frequently do you climax? Is there pain or discomfort associated with intercourse?)

Do you feel that both you and your husband (wife) are equally adventurous sexually (i.e., interested in trying new things with each other), or is one of you more so than the other?

Since your marriage, have you been tempted or actually been involved with anyone else?

For some couples, sex is the center of their relationship; for others it is important but no more important than other aspects of the marriage. How do you see the place of sex in your marriage?

4. Relationship with Family of Origin

Tell me about the family you grew up in (what it was like).

Tell me about your mother: what was she like? Your father: what was he like? What was their relationship like?

Tell me about your siblings and your relationship with them.

What was your relationship like to your mother? Your father? What was your role in the family as you were growing up? (the student, the quiet one, the go-between, etc.)

What do you think were the real strengths of your family?

What were the real stresses in your family?

As you approach parenting, do you want to be the same kind of parent your parents were? Did you have any "special" relationships in the family? Whom were you closest to? Whom did you have the most trouble with?

What is your relationship like now with your family? Your mother? Father? Siblings? Do you see them often? Call them often?

How much financial support, if any, do you get from them? *(ask about gifts such as cars, furniture, clothes etc., as well as money)*

How much emotional support, if any, do you get from them?

How much of a personal stress to you is your family? In what ways?

How does your family respond to your husband (wife)?

How does he (she) respond to them?

5. Hopes/Fears About Pregnancy and Child

How did you feel about your (wife's) pregnancy?

First pregnancy or previous miscarriages?

Were you trying to get pregnant, or did it just happen? Any ambivalence?

How has the pregnancy affected your relationship with your spouse?

All parents seem to have hopes and fears about the pregnancy, delivery, and child. What have yours been? How much have you thought about what the child will be like?

Do you have any secret preferences for either a boy or a girl? Do you think your husband (wife) does?

How do you feel about your OB doctor?

How has your family responded to your (wife's) pregnancy?

Have you attended or do you plan to attend prenatal or Lamaze classes?

6. Perception of Self

I want to get an idea of what it's like to be you. How do you experience yourself? What are you like? *(usually must encourage subject)*

Do you feel mostly the same from day to day and week to week, or are there pretty distinct changes in you from time to time?

Let me ask you about some specific aspects of your personality. Think of a graph with extremes at each end and tell me where you think you fit best.

1. Outgoing, extroverted vs quiet, shy?
2. Aggressive, initiating vs more passive and following?
3. Trusting or cautious?
4. Impulsive or highly controlled?
5. Intellectual or feeling?
6. Highly social or tend to isolate?
7. Usually serious or more fun-loving?
8. Usually confident or more insecure?
9. Usually pleased with self or usually critical of self?
10. Enjoy competition or avoid competition?
11. Warm or more distant?
12. Mostly present-oriented or mostly future-oriented?

Do you use alcohol, tobacco, marijuana (or other drugs) and, if so, how much? How about in the past?

Are you taking any prescription drugs for tension, mood, or sleeping problems?

How much anxiety do you experience? Severity? *(interference with work, pleasure)* Episodic or long-lasting? Specific antecedents or free-floating?

How much depression do you experience? Severity? (interfere with work or pleasure). Duration? Ever wish you were dead? Suicide thoughts, attempts?

Have you had many physical symptoms for which doctors can find no physical cause?

Have you ever experienced a serious emotional disturbance? Did it require therapy or counseling? Medication? Hospitalization?

How satisfied are you with your life? Do you usually think of yourself as emotionally healthy?

APPENDIX 1b.

Time 3:
Individual Interview (Three Months)

1. Child and Child Care

Describe (baby). What's he/she like?

Is he/she a happy/fussy baby?
What are his/her schedules like?
How is he/she sleeping?
How is he/she eating? (Still breast feeding? When stopped?. What was that like? On solid food? When started solids? Why? What was that like?)

What's it like to take care of (baby)?

How do you feel about being a parent now that (baby) is 3 months old?
How does he/she respond when you dress, bathe him/her?
Has he/she been ill much? What was that like?
Does he/she often play/amuse himself/herself, or do you have to entertain him/her quite a bit?
Does he/she like to go to new places? How does he/she react?
Do you see bits and pieces of others (relatives) in (baby's) personality?

(For mothers who have quit work.)

How does caring for a child compare with working outside the home?
Do you plan to resume work? When? How was that decision made?
How do you feel about that?
What arrangements will you make for child care?

(For husbands of mothers who have not resumed employment.)

From your perception, how does (wife) like caring for a child as opposed to working outside the home?
Does she plan to resume work? When? How was that decision made?
How do you feel about it?
What arrangements will you make for child care?

(For mothers who have resumed employment; ask both wife and husband.)

How have you managed child care, etc.?
How do you feel about it?
How has (baby) responded?
How has your work been affected by being a parent?

2. Marital Relationship

Tell me what your relationship with (spouse) has been like since (baby) was born.

Has it been a good time or a difficult time for the two of you?
Do you find that you have much time to talk about everyday events (world, work, etc.)?
Do you find that you talk about everyday feelings (hurt, anger)?
Do you find that you talk about more private, inner feelings, (fears, thoughts, feelings that are private, vulnerable)?
Has there been more or less conflict than before (baby) was born?
What has decision-making been like recently? How do you make decisions?
How openly affectionate are you with each other now? Have there been any changes?

Tell me about your sexual relationship.

Have you resumed sexual relations since (baby's) birth?
If no, have you talked about when you will resume them?

How do you feel about that?

If yes, when did you resume them? How did you decide to resume them? How was your response when you resumed? Your spouse's?
Are there changes in your sexual relationship from before the pregnancy? How do you feel about those?
Wife — Have you had, are you having any pain or discomfort with sexual relations?
Husband — Do you perceive that (wife) has had or is having any pain or discomfort with sexual relations?

3. Friendship Network

Has your relationship with your friends changed since (baby's) birth? How do you feel about it?
Do you have friends who help you out (baby-sitting, advice, etc.)?

4. Family of Origin

Tell me how your family has reacted to (baby's) birth?
How do you feel about their reaction to (baby's) birth?
How has spouse's family reacted to (baby's) birth?
How do you feel about their reaction to (baby's) birth?
Have they visited? How often? Call? How often?
Has your relationship with your parents changed since birth? (spouse's parents?)
In what ways have they been helpful? In what ways have they been a stress?
Do they assist in child care? How often? Would you like more or less help from them?

5. Perception of Self

How have your feelings about yourself changed over the last few months?
Let's talk about how you have experienced yourself over the last few months.

What has it been like to be you?
How satisfied do you feel with yourself right now?
Do you sense any specific changes in you since (baby's) birth?
Sometimes as we grow older, we see more and more of our parents in ourselves; how much of your father, your mother, do you experience in yourself?
How much anxiety have you experienced in the last few months? Severity? *(interference with work, pleasure)* Episodic or long-lasting? Specific antecedents or free floating?
How much depression have you experienced in the last few months? Severity? *(interference with work or pleasure)* Duration? Ever wish you were dead? Suicidal thoughts, attempts?
Have there been any changes in your physical health since the child was born?
Have you had any illness in the last few months? Any physical symptoms for which doctors could not find a physical cause?
Do you feel you've been mostly the same from day to day and week to week, or have there been pretty distinct changes in you from time to time?
Are you using alcohol, tobacco, marijuana (or other drugs), and if so, how much?
Are you taking any prescription drugs for tension, mood, or sleeping problems?
Has anyone who knows you well picked up any changes in you since the baby was born?

APPENDIX 1c.

Time 4:
Individual Interview (One Year)

Fill me in on what's been going on in your life since we talked to you last.

What's changed in your life?

Have there been major changes in work, your health, your relationship with your spouse or your family?

Looking over the time since we last talked, what stands out as important?

1. Parent-Child Relations

We haven't seen you since (baby) was three months old. What have things been like for you? What have been the major satisfactions of being a parent? The major concerns?

How satisfied are you with being a parent? What does it mean to you to be a parent? What kind of a parent have you been?

What kind of parent has (spouse) been? How much does he/she enjoy it? How involved is he/she with baby?

What kinds of things do you do with (baby)? What do you especially enjoy? What do you find tedious?

What sort of baby has (baby) been?

As babies go, and they differ a lot, is (baby) a very demanding baby?

Does (baby) remind you of someone in the family? Who is he/she most like?

Does (baby) show strong preferences for certain people? Are there things he/she would rather have you do with him/her than mother/father/babysitter? Are there things he/she would rather have spouse do?

What is it like now for you to leave baby in someone else's care? Does it worry you? How do you feel? Does baby show any signs of being upset when you leave? Why do you think this happens? How does he/she react when you return?

Does (baby) do as you ask right away, or do you have to ask him/her several times before he does it?

Does (baby) do many things that you think he/she should know better than to do?

Does (baby) play with his/her own toys a lot, or does he/she get into things that don't belong to him/her? How do you handle that?

At what time is (baby) most difficult to deal with—mealtimes, bedtimes, bathtimes? What's that like?

Does (baby) follow you around and hang on to you? How do you react when he/she does that?

Does (baby) go to sleep easily? What are bedtimes like?

Does (baby) sleep through the night? How often does he/she wake up? What happens when he/she wakes up?

How often do you take (baby) into your bed or sleep in his/her bed because he/she is upset?

Does (baby) feed himself/herself? What's that like?

Is (baby) an active child compared to other 1-year-olds you have seen? When is he/she most active?

Does (baby) play at one activity for long periods of time, or does he/she change activities often? What's the longest time?

Does (baby) ever climb up on tables, cupboards? What do you say or do?

Some parents expect children to obey immediately when they tell them something; others don't think that it's so terribly important. How do you feel about this?

How does your spouse feel about strict obedience?

How do you react when (baby) does what you ask right away?

If (baby) doesn't do what you ask, do you ever drop the subject or do you always see that (baby) does it?

What are the things that you insist he/she not do?

If (baby) does something you don't approve of, what do you do? Give me an example.

How much time do you spend playing with (baby) each day?

Would you describe (baby) as an affectionate child?

Do you keep track of exactly where (baby) is and what he/she is doing, or can you let him/her entertain himself/herself for long periods of time?

Is your yard enclosed? Do you ever let (baby) play in the yard alone without checking? For how long?

How much time do you spend holding or cuddling (baby)?

How has (baby's) health been? Any illnesses or medically attended accidents?

How do you and your spouse divide up childrearing tasks? Who disciplines, cuddles, consoles, bathes, feeds, plays with, puts to bed, reads stories? Is that what you had planned in terms of dividing things up before the baby came?

Do you perceive (spouse) as helpful and supportive in raising (baby)? Do you disagree quite a bit about how to raise him/her, or mostly agree? How do you feel about that? Are there differences in the way you discipline or respond to (baby)?

What is a typical family day like for you? Do the same things happen at the same time, or does it change quite a bit? Do you try to keep things constant? How does (baby) react to changes in schedule?

What are your plans at this point about having another baby?

2. Marital Relations

What is the most important aspect of your marriage? How has it been for you and (spouse) as a couple since we last talked? What's changed, what's remained the same? Looking back at the first year of being a mother/father, how do you think having a baby has changed your relationship?

How satisfied are you now with your relationship with (spouse)?

Have you found yourself reevaluating your marriage — questioning your marriage choice at all? Have you found yourself considering becoming involved in an extramarital relationship? Has that happened?

How close do you feel you are? What makes it close? Have there been any changes in closeness for the two of you? How well do you think (spouse) understands what being a parent has been like for you? Have you discussed this?

Have you found that the parent-child relationship conflicts with your marital relationship? How have you handled that? Have you discussed that together?

How often do you and (spouse) get time just for the two of you?

When did you start finding that time (age of child)? Have you both tried to make the time, or has one been more active than the other in trying to arrange times for the two of you to be alone? *(get specific information about how frequently they get babysitters and go out and at whose initiation)*

How satisfied are you with the way decisions are made? How are they made? Any disagreements? How are these resolved?

Are there any particular areas of conflict between the two of you? What are these? How often do these issues come up? Have you been able to resolve these issues?

How satisfied are you with sexual relations now? How frequently? Any changes?

3. Family of Origin

Since we have talked to you last, how have things been in your relationship to your family and your in-laws? Tell me about your parents' and in-laws' reaction to the baby.

How has having a baby changed your relationship with your family of origin? Do you feel the same ties, closer ties, or more distant to them than before? Do you see them more or less? More involved in each other's lives or less involved? How about your in-laws?

How about your spouse? How has his/her relationship changed to his/her parents and family? Are the ties the same, closer, or more distant? Does he/she see them more or less? Are they more involved in each other's lives or less involved? How do you feel about that?

How about your spouse and your parents? *(same questions)*

Do you find yourself re-evaluating your relationship to your parents, or re-evaluating your perception of your parents? Tell me about that.

What kinds of things do your parents and in-laws do with the baby; how involved are they, how much help are they, how much stress are they?

How does your current family compare with the family you grew up in?

4. Religion

Have there been any changes in the role of religion in your lives?

Have there been any disagreements about the role of religion?

5. Work*

Tell me what's happened in your work since we last talked.

Have you found yourself re-evaluating where you are in work?

How satisfied are you with your work and your career?

How well is work going for you? Any special successes, disappointments?

How well is work fitting in with family life?

How satisfied have you been with the time and energy you've had for your spouse? For your baby?

Does work give you enough flexibility to meet family obligations?

How much time are you able to spend with child and spouse?

(For mothers who have gone back to work between three months and one year, ask both wife and husband.)

How do you feel about (wife's) being away from the baby for work?

Do you enjoy work? Resent being away from the baby?

How do you perceive that it's affected the baby?

How have you managed substitute child care? How do you feel about the child care? How has the baby responded?

Tell me what the first few weeks were like after you went back to work.

(For mothers who were working at three months — ask husbands too.)

How do you feel about (wife's) being away from the baby for work?

Do you enjoy work or resent being away from the baby?

How do you perceive that it has affected the baby?

---

*Several of the interview questions were taken from an interview by E. Hock, K. Christman, and M. Hock (1980), Factors associated with decisions about return to work in mothers of infants. *Developmental Psychology 16* (5), 535-536.

Are you using the same child care as you were at three months? (changes, how many, why). How do you feel about the child care you're receiving?

How has the baby responded?

(For mothers who aren't working.)

How do you feel about not working? Do you miss it? Do you enjoy being at home? If you were working now, would you enjoy it or resent it?

How does caring for a child compare with working outside the home?

Do you plan to resume work? When? If yes, what arrangement will you make for child care?

(Ask husbands.)

How do you perceive wife feels about not working? Do you think she misses it? Do you think she would enjoy working or resent it right now? How do you feel about her not working?

Does she plan to resume work? When? How do you feel about that?

6. Feelings About Self

How have you experienced yourself, felt about yourself, since we've seen you last? Have you found yourself re-evaluating what's important to you or where your life is going?

How satisfied are you now with yourself and where your life is going? Do you sense any changes since the baby's birth?

How do you feel about your physical self?

How much anxiety have you experienced over the last nine months? Enough to interfere with work or pleasure? Episodic or long-lasting? Specific antecedents or free-floating? Changes in anxiety level?

How much depression have you experienced in the last few months? Severity? Enough to interfere with work or pleasure? Duration? Ever wish you were dead, have suicidal thoughts, or made suicidal attempts?

How much have you experienced elation or strong feelings of well-being? More or less than in the past?

Have there been changes in your physical health since your child was born? Any illnesses in the last nine months?

Do you feel you've been mostly the same day to day, week to week, or have there been distinct changes?

Are you using alcohol, tobacco, marijuana, any other drugs—how much? Changes in last nine months?

Are you taking prescription drugs for tension, mood, or sleeping problems?

On the whole, have the last nine months been a good time for you or one of the more difficult times in your life?

APPENDIX 2a.

Time 1: Marital Interview (Prenatal)

1. Experience of Pregnancy

What has the pregnancy been like for both of you?

How did you feel when you learned that you were pregnant? *(Ask both individually)*

How has your pregnancy been thus far? (Sickness, nausea, vomiting?) Any other difficulties?

When is your due date? How do you feel about the changes in your body? (Weight gain, changes in shape?) (Bothersome?) What do you think it will be like in the last month when you really get big? *(Ask husband how he feels)*

How much has the pregnancy changed your activities? (Has it interfered with things you like to do?)

2. Anticipation of Changes

Let's talk about your anticipation of changes.

How do you think having a baby will change your life?
As a couple?
Husband: How do you think it will change your life?
Wife: How do you think it will change your life? (Are you going to work outside the home?)

How are you going to manage child care? How will it be divided? Who will do what? Have you thought about whether you will breast or bottle feed? How did you make the decision?

Husband: What child care do you imagine you will do? (Feeding, getting up during the night, etc.) What do you think that will be like for you?

Have you read any books on child care?

Have you talked about how you will respond to the child? (When he/she cries, feed when it wants or on a schedule, when do you think you'll start disciplining, what age?)

What are your expectations of the child? What problems do you expect? What will be fun?

3. Religion

Let's talk some about the role of religion in your lives.

Tell me about the role, if any, that religion plays in your life.

What are your religious backgrounds?

What role did religion play in your family when you were growing up?

Have differences in religious backgrounds presented problems or conflicts for you? (Tell me about that.)

Did it affect your decision to get married? *(If yes to above)* Are there any ongoing conflicts about religion?

Do you attend church now? (Both of you, which church, how regularly, since marriage or recently?)

Is religion a part of your everyday life? (Prayer, etc.)

What effect has expecting a child had on your view of church attendance, the role of religion, etc?

Do you intend to have the child baptized or christened?

Have there been any problems about deciding on religious training for the child, baptism, etc.?

4. History of the Relationship

Let's talk about the history of your relationship.

Tell me when and how you met.

What attracted you to each other?

How long did you know each other (go together) prior to your marriage? When did you get serious?

What was your engagement like (formal, length)?

For many couples, deciding when to begin sexual relationships is an issue that needs to be resolved.

Was this a difficult issue in your relationship? Did you have sexual relations prior to marriage?

Did you live together prior to marriage? *(If yes)* Was this a difficult issue? Were you able to tell your parents and friends that you were living together?

For many couples, the early years of marriage can be smooth or stormy. What have yours been like? Has there been a lot of conflict? Has either of you ever walked out after an argument? (Tell me about that—how often, how long, who left?)

Has either of you ever mentioned divorce? How serious were you? Did you pursue it? How often has this happened?

When you married, did you plan to have children? (How many? Was this pregnancy planned? If so, how long did it take you to get pregnant? Do you plan to have more children? What spacing would you like? How many?)

5. Money Management

Let's talk some about how you manage money.

Would you both discuss how you manage money?

Do you have a budget? (If not formal, do you have a household allowance, clothing allowance, gift purchasing, or do you just buy what you need?)

Who manages money? How is it managed? (Give spouse certain amount, etc.)

Do you have disagreements about money management? How money should be spent? Do you find that you have similar or different priorities for ways that money is spent?

Who determines how money is spent? Is it a source of conflict? When was the last time? Describe for me what happened.

Have you both worked since your marriage? Do you pool money to meet your expenses? One checking account or two? Have you always had that arrangement?

Almost all couples find that it takes many years after marriage to feel that they are financially secure. It seems particularly hard to save money or make investments in the early years of marriage, and almost all couples find that they have debts.

How would you assess your financial situation? Loans or debts? (Car loans, house mortgages, educational debts, credit card balances due, etc.) Does this concern you? Do you feel your debts are manageable?

How about savings? Have you been able to save? For any particular purpose? Have investments? Who decides this?

Often, in early marriage, couples just make it month to month? How do things go month to month for you? Are you able to save a little each month, just make it, or overdraw sometimes? How often?

Is this a good time financially to have a baby? Does that ever worry you?

Do you have any financial help from your families? What kind, how much, from whom? If yes, who decides how the money from the family is spent?

How do you shop? Only when you need things or do you use shopping as entertainment? Do you ever buy things you didn't intend to buy?

Are you from similar or different economic backgrounds?

How has getting married influenced your financial situation?

6. Value Differences

Let's talk about the value survey that you both did.

Why don't you both read off your top five terminal values *(Rokeach Value Survey)?* Now, how about the bottom five?

Are there any surprises for either of you?

You seem to have (a) lots of differences; there are (b) a few differences; there are (c) hardly any differences. Does this surprise you? What did you think about that? What did you think of the value of the survey? In general, do you think having similar values is important in a marriage?

7. Life Dream

Let's talk about what we call life dreams.

Many people have a life dream, a daydream of what they want their life to be like, a sort of secret dream that we have about what our life should be, what it should mean. It's sometimes hard for us to talk about our dreams, but it seems we all have some.

Do either of you have such a dream — either an individual or a shared dream concerning what you hope your life will be about under the best circumstances? If a shared dream, whose dream is it?

What would you have liked to have done about your life in 10, 20, 30 years — what would you like to be like?

Have you talked about these dreams?

If each has a dream, has one person's dream taken precedence over the other?

In what ways has your spouse been supportive of your dream? How supportive? Is one more supportive than the other? You've told me a lot about your marriage, your life, your expectations of your child; is there anything that is important that I haven't asked?

APPENDIX 2b.

Time 3:
Marital Interview (Three Months)

1. Child and Child Care

What have the last three months with (baby) been like for both of you (individually, as a couple)?

Has it been what you expected?

What have been the good things?

What have been the problems?

It is sometimes hard for couples to work out how they are going to share housework, child care, work, bill paying, all of the tasks. How have the two of you done? Do you feel things have gone smoothly or roughly during the last three months?

How do you handle child care? Who does what?

Do you ever disagree about what to do for the baby, or how to handle a specific situation? Can you remember a time? Tell me what happened?

How have you handled feedings?

What do you do when (baby) cries — go to him/her immediately or let him/her cry for a while?

Have there been any disagreements about how to respond to (baby)?

If you have a question about how to deal with the baby, what do you do? Ask pediatrician, consult book, consult friends, consult relatives, decide yourselves?

How many times have you called the pediatrician about problems? What were they? Who called? Did you both agree that you needed to call?

2. Marital Relationships

For many couples, the period of adjustment after the birth of a child can be difficult or fairly easy. Considering your relationship with each other, have things gone more smoothly or more roughly in the last three months?

What specific disagreements have there been?

Has there been more or less conflict? Any arguments where one of you has walked out? Tell me about that — what about, how often, how long, who left.

Have you had any misgivings about the stability of the relationship?

3. Future Children

How do you feel about more children now? How many more, how soon? Do you agree on this?

Are you using contraceptives now? What kind? Do you intend to start using them? What kind, when?

4. Values

Do you think your values have changed since the birth of (baby)?

5. Life Dream

How has having a child changed the way you see your life going in the next 10, 20, 30 years?

If so, in what way has that changed?

APPENDIX 3.

Marital
Interaction Discussion Tasks

Time 1 (Prenatal)

Task 1. During the next eight minutes we would like the two of you to imagine that your economic situation has become so bad that the two of you must live with one of your families. Please discuss with each other whose family you would choose to live with, why you would make that choice, and what you would see as the consequences.

Task 2. Please discuss what have been the most pleasurable aspects of your marriage and what have been the painful aspects of your marriage.

Task 3. First, please see if the two of you can agree on what is the greatest source of disagreement in your marriage and second, see if you can make any progress towards resolving that disagreement in the next eight minutes.

Task 4. During the last task we ask that you plan an activity together. The activity can be something that you would do and should involve both of you.

Time 3 (Three Months)

Task 1. For the first couple interaction task, please discuss the best and the worst aspects of being a parent.

Task 2. For the next couple interaction task, please discuss the positive and negative changes that have occurred in your marital relationship since the birth of your child.

Task 3. For the last couple interaction, please discuss the things that you think married couples should know before having their first child.

Time 4 (One year)

Task 1. For the first discussion, we would like the two of you to discuss what each of you thinks your individual strengths and weaknesses as a parent are and what you think your spouse's individual strengths and weaknesses as a parent are. Then try to make some progress toward agreeing on what each of your individual strengths and weaknesses are as parents.

Task 2. For the second discussion, we would like the two of you to discuss with each other what you really like or what really feels good to you about your interactions with your spouse. What are your problems? What does not feel so good to you about your interactions with your spouse? Please take turns telling each other what you especially like about the way you and your spouse interact with each other. And then take turns telling each other what are problems for you in the way you and your spouse interact with each other or what doesn't feel so good about your interactions.

Task 3. For the last couple discussion, we would like the two of you to discuss between you the current major source of disagreement in your marriage and see if you can make some progress toward resolving that disagreement.

APPENDIX 4.

Family of Origin Questionnaire

The questions on the next few pages concern your perceptions of your relationships and experiences while growing up. Underneath each question, circle the number (1 through 5) that best describes your perception. There are no right or wrong answers; your perception is what is important.

For example: In the first question, if you think your mother had a great deal of anxiety about fulfilling her role as mother, circle 1; if her anxiety was high, but not disruptively high, circle 2; if it was moderate, circle 3; if she had some, but not much anxiety, circle 4; and if she had little or no anxiety, circle 5. Proceed in a similar way with the other questions. We have some questions on the next few pages about your perception of your own mother and how she handled the maternal role as you were growing up.

1. How anxious do you think your mother was about fulfilling her role as a mother?

1	2	3	4	5
Extremely anxious		Moderate anxiety		Little or no anxiety

2. How sensitive was your mother to your needs as a child; how much was she able to understand your feelings?

1	2	3	4	5
Insensitive even when told about your needs		Aware of varying needs and moods		Very sensitive and aware (even with minimal cues)

3. How close was your mother to you when you were a child?

1	2	3	4	5
Distant		Close		Very close

4. How much did your mother intrude into your life and independence?

1	2	3	4	5
Intense, aggressive involvement		Moderate intrusion		Little or no intrusion on individuality

5. How did you mother react to her maternal role?

1	2	3	4	5
Actively resented the demands	Disappointed frustrated	Ambivalent	Satisfied	Extremely happy with her maternal role

6. The extent to which your mother satisfied your emotional needs from infancy through age 12.

1	2	3	4	5
Support needs essentially unmet	Rarely met	Support needs sometimes met	Usually met	Support needs essentially met

7. The extent to which your mother satisfied your emotional needs after age 12.

1	2	3	4	5
Support needs essentially unmet	Rarely met	Support needs sometimes met	Usually met	Support needs essentially met

We have some questions on the next few pages about your perception of your own father and how he handled the paternal role as you were growing up.

1. How anxious do you think your father was about fulfilling his role as a father?

1	2	3	4	5
Extremely anxious		Moderate anxiety		Little or no anxiety

2. How sensitive was your father to your needs as a child; how much was he able to understand your feelings?

1	2	3	4	5
Insensitive even when told about your needs		Aware of varying needs and moods		Very sensitive and aware (even with minimal cues)

3. How close was your father to you when you were a child?

1	2	3	4	5
Distant		Close		Very close

4. How much did your father intrude into your life and independence?

1	2	3	4	5
Intense, aggressive involvement		Moderate intrusion		Little or no intrusion on individuality

5. How did your father react to his paternal role?

1	2	3	4	5
Actively resented the demands	Disappointed frustrated	Ambivalent	Satisfied	Extremely happy with his paternal role

6. The extent to which your father satisfied your emotional needs from infancy through age 12.

1	2	3	4	5
Support needs essentially unmet	Rarely met	Support needs sometimes met	Usually met	Support needs essentially met

7. The extent to which your father satisfied your emotional needs after age 12.

1	2	3	4	5
Support needs essentially unmet	Rarely met	Support needs sometimes met	Usually met	Support needs essentially met

Now we would like to ask some questions about your perceptions of your parents' marriage during your childhood. For each question, please check the statement that best describes your parents' relationship.

1. How were decisions made in your family?

   Father always made decisions _____

   Mother always made decisions _____

   Father made final decision but listened to mother _____

   Mother made final decision but listened to father _____

   Mother and father made decisions together _____

   No one really made decisions; it was hard to get decisions made _____

2. How close were your parents to each other when you were growing up?

   Very close _____

   Somewhat close _____

   Not very close _____

   Led completely independent lives _____

3. To what degree did your parents openly express feelings toward each other?

   Openly and directly expressed feelings _____

   Direct expression of feelings with some discomfort _____

   Some restriction of feelings _____

   Some feelings expressed, most not _____

   No expression of feelings _____

4. Rate the overall mood and tone of your parents' interactions with each other.

   Usually warm, affectionate, humorous, and optimistic _____

   Polite, without much warmth or affection _____

   Frequently hostile with a few pleasant times _____

   Very hostile _____

   Depressed _____

   Cynical, hopeless, pessimistic _____

5. Rate the degree to which you perceived your parents as having unresolvable conflict.

   Severe conflict _____

   Definite conflict that disrupted family _____

Some conflict that somewhat disrupted family _____

Some conflict but not disruptive to family _____

Little or no conflict _____

6. Rate the degree to which your parents were sensitive to and understanding of each other's feelings.

Consistently sensitive and understanding with each other _____

Usually sensitive and understanding _____

Tried to be, but failed usually _____

Were never sensitive and understanding with each other _____

Reacted totally inappropriately to each others' feelings _____

APPENDIX 5.

Beavers-Timberlawn
Family Evaluation Scale

BEAVERS-TIMBERLAWN FAMILY EVALUATION SCALE

Family Name ....

Segment ....

Rater ....

Date ....

Instructions: The following scales were designed to assess the family functioning on continua representing interactional aspects of being a family. Therefore, it is important that you consider the entire range of each scale when you make your ratings. Please try to *respond on the basis of the videotape data alone*, scoring according to what you see and hear, rather than what you imagine might occur elsewhere.

I. *Structure of the Family*

A. Overt Power: Based on the entire tape, check the term that best describes your general impression of the overt power relationships of this family.

1	1.5	2	2.5	3	3.5	4	4.5	5
Chaos		Marked dominance		Moderate dominance		Led		Egalitarian
Leaderless; no one has enough power to structure the inter-action.		Control is close to absolute. No nego-tiation; dominance and submission are the rule.		Control is close to absolute. Some nego-tiation, but dominance and submission are the rule.		Tendency toward dom-inance and submission, but most of the inter-action is through respectful negotiation.		Leadership is shared between parents, changing with the nature of the interaction.

(continued)

157

B. Parental Coalitions: Check the terms that best describe the relationship structure in this family.

1	1.5	2	2.5	3	3.5	4	4.5	5
Parent-child coalition				Weak parental coalition				Strong parental coalition

C. Closeness

1	1.5	2	2.5	3	3.5	4	4.5	5
Amorphous, vague and indistinct boundaries among members				Isolation, distancing				Closeness, with distinct boundaries among members

II. *Mythology:* Every family has a mythology; that is, a concept of how it functions as a group. Rate the degree to which this family's mythology seems congruent with reality.

1	1.5	2	2.5	3	3.5	4	4.5	5
Very congruent		Mostly congruent				Somewhat incongruent		Very incongruent

III. *Goal-Directed Negotiation:* Rate this family's overall efficiency in negotiating problem solutions.

1	1.5	2	2.5	3	3.5	4	4.5	5
Extremely efficient		Good				Poor		Extremely inefficient

(continued)

IV. Autonomy

A. **Clarity of Expression:** Rate this family as to the clarity of disclosure of feelings and thoughts. This is not a rating of the intensity or variety of feelings, but rather of clarity of individual thoughts and feelings.

1	1.5	2	2.5	3	3.5	4	4.5	5
Very clear				Somewhat vague and hidden				Hardly anyone is ever clear

B. **Responsibility:** Rate the degree to which the family members take responsibility for their own past, present, and future actions.

1	1.5	2	2.5	3	3.5	4	4.5	5
Members regularly are able to voice responsibility for individual actions				Members sometimes voice responsibility for individual actions, but tactics also include sometimes blaming others, speaking in 3rd person or plural				Members rarely, if ever, voice responsibility for individual actions

C. **Invasiveness:** Rate the degree to which the members speak for one another, or make "mind reading" statements.

1	1.5	2	2.5	3	3.5	4	4.5	5
Many invasions				Occasional invasions				No evidence of invasions

(continued)

D. Permeability: Rate the degree to which members are open, receptive and permeable to the statements of other family members.

1	1.5	2	2.5	3	3.5	4	4.5	5
Very open		Moderately open				Members frequently unreceptive		Members unreceptive

V. Family Affect

A. Range of Feelings: Rate the degree to which this family system is characterized by a wide range expression of feelings.

1	1.5	2	2.5	3	3.5	4	4.5	5
Direct expression of a wide range of feelings		Direct expression of many feelings despite some difficulty		Obvious restriction in the expressions of some feelings		Although some feelings are expressed, there is masking of most feelings		Little or no expression of feelings

B. Mood and Tone: Rate the feeling tone of this family's interaction.

1	1.5	2	2.5	3	3.5	4	4.5	5
Usually warm, affectionate, humorous and optimistic		Polite, without impressive warmth or affection; or frequently hostile with times of pleasure		Overtly hostile		Depressed		Cynical, hopeless and pessimistic

(continued)

160

C. Unresolvable Conflict: Rate the degree of seemingly unresolvable conflict.

1	1.5	2	2.5	3	3.5	4	4.5	5
Severe conflict, with severe impairment of group functioning		Definite conflict, with moderate impairment of group functioning			Definite conflict, with slight impairment of group functioning	Some evidence of unresolvable conflict, without impairment of group functioning		Little, or no unresolvable conflict

D. Empathy: Rate the degree of sensitivity to, and understanding of, each other's feelings within this family.

1	1.5	2	2.5	3	3.5	4	4.5	5
Consistent empathic responsiveness		For the most part, an empathic responsiveness with one another, despite obvious resistance		Attempted empathic involvement, but failed to maintain it		Absence of any empathic responsiveness		Grossly inappropriate responses to feelings

VI. *Global Health-Pathology Scale:* *Circle the number* of the point on the following scale that best describes this family's health or pathology.

10	9	8	7	6	5	4	3	2	1
Most Pathological									Healthiest

APPENDIX 6a.

Marital Competence Scoring Sheet

Family _____

Date _____

Rater _____

Sources

Individual Interviews

Marital Interviews

Marital Interaction Tasks

MRI

Role Survey

Please circle ratings
1a. *Power*
   1. Chaotic
   2. Predominantly conflicted
   3. Markedly dominant
   4. Moderately dominant
   5. Led
   6. Egalitarian
1b. *Satisfaction with distribution of power*
   1. Very satisfied
   2. Somewhat satisfied
   3. Somewhat dissatisfied
   4. Very dissatisfied
2a. *Intimacy of communication*
   1. Not able to discuss private vulnerable feelings or thoughts
   2. Discuss private vulnerable feelings only with great difficulty

3. Some difficulty discussing private feelings, perhaps more one than another
4. Great ability to discuss anything, including very private personal feelings

2b. Satisfaction with intimacy
1. Very satisfied
2. Somewhat satisfied
3. Somewhat dissatisfied
4. Very satisfied

3a. Closeness
1. Not at all close; very few shared perceptions, beliefs, values, activities, or friendships; little affection; little mutual respect, appreciation, or shared humor
2.
3. Somewhat close
4.
5. Very close; shared perceptions, beliefs, values, activities, and friendships; much affection; considerable mutual respect, appreciation, shared humor

3b. Satisfaction with closeness
1. Very dissatisfied
2. Somewhat dissatisfied
3. Somewhat dissatisfied
4. Very satisfied

4a. Commitment to enduring marriage
1. Evidence of a very strong investment or commitment
2. Evidence of a somewhat strong investment or commitment
3. Evidence of a somewhat weak investment or commitment
4. Evidence of a very weak investment or commitment

4b. Separation from family of origin
W H
1. 1. Little separation, individual is still greatly involved with family of origin with evidence of some negative affect or extreme dependence
2. 2.
3. 3. Optimal separation, warm relationship with f.o., some contact but clear respect and independence in f.o. relationship
4. 4.
5. 5. Distance from f.o., negative affect, or lack of warmth

4c. Satisfaction with separation from family of origin
W H
1. 1. Very satisfied
2. 2. Somewhat satisfied
3. 3. Somewhat dissatisfied
4. 4. Very dissatisfied

APPENDIX 6b.

The Continuum
of Marital Competence

1	2	3	4	5	6	7	8	9	10

Highly competent	Competent but pained	Complementary dominant-submissive	Conflicted	Severely dysfunc- tional

Highly Competent

1. Egalitarian power relationships with very high levels of closeness, high levels of intimacy, a very strong commitment to the marital relationship as the central interpersonal alliance, and very high levels of satisfaction.

2. Several patterns can be seen here. One is an egalitarian power relationship and very high levels of closeness, but with some difficulty in achieving intimacy with a very strong commitment to the relationship and either high levels of satisfaction or very high levels of satisfaction. A second pattern is a pattern of one spouse providing leadership to the marriage with either high levels of intimacy or some difficulty in achieving intimacy, but with a very strong commitment and either high or very high levels of satisfaction.

Competent but Pained

3. One spouse provides leadership and the couple is close. There is some to great difficulty, however, in achieving intimacy. Commitment can be either somewhat strong, strong, or very strong and there is a variable level of satisfaction with the relationship.

4. The relationship can be either egalitarian, one in which leadership of one spouse is apparent, or one in which one spouse is moderately dominant. In the egalitarian type, there is some closeness, great difficulty with intimacy, and only a somewhat strong commitment to the relationship and moderate levels of dissatisfaction with certain aspects of the relationship. In the leadership pattern there is not very much closeness, great difficulty with intimacy, a somewhat strong commitment to the relationship, and somewhat or moderate levels of satisfaction with the relationship. In the type of relationship in which one spouse is moderately dominant, the level of closeness can range from somewhat close to very close, and there is either some or great difficulty achieving intimacy and the pattern of commitment can range from somewhat to very strong. There is, however, a variable level of satisfaction with the relationship.

Complementary Dominant-Submissive

5. Moderately dominated relationship without obvious conflict in which the spouses are close but do not achieve intimacy but have a very strong commitment to the relationship and high levels of satisfaction.
6. Another moderately dominated relationship with some evidence of hidden conflict with midrange levels of closeness, and with either great difficulty achieving intimacy or the absence of intimacy in the relationship. The range of commitment can be from low to very strong, and the range of satisfaction with the relationship can range from dissatisfied to somewhat satisfied.

Conflicted

7. There is a clear pattern of dominance but the relationship is characterized more by the conflict between the spouses. There is either no closeness or little closeness. Intimacy is not achieved and the degree of commitment to the relationship may range from low to very strong. There is also considerable variation in the amount of satisfaction running from dissatisfaction to moderate levels of satisfaction.
8. Here, although there may be attempts at dominance, conflict is the central issue. There is little in the way of closeness and no intimacy or great difficulty achieving it, and there is a weak commitment and moderate to high levels of dissatisfaction.
9. A severely conflicted, disorganized, and in some ways chaotic relationship with no closeness, no intimacy and a very weak commitment to the relationship with high levels of dissatisfaction. This type of relationship can be seen as verging on dissolution of the relationship.

Severely Dysfunctional

10. A truly merged or fused relationship in which conflict is absent or minimal because each partner has sacrificed individuality. As a consequence they are seen as very close, although the degree of fusion and sameness makes the communication of intimate feelings impossible. There is a very strong commitment to the relationship and a high level of satisfaction.

or

A relationship that is dominated by one spouse's psychosis (frequently paranoid) and the other spouse's acceptance of those distortions of reality. They may seem very close although individuality is sacrificed. Strong commitment and high satisfaction is usually seen.

or

An alienated relationship in which the spouses live together without emotional contact with each other. Anger is infrequent, closeness and intimacy absent, and commitment ranges from absent to moderate.

APPENDIX 7a.

Time 3:
Parental Involvement Ratings*

(From Individual Interview)

Parent's Delight in the Baby

When a parent is delighted with his/her baby, he/she not only feels great pleasure but he/she is capable of expressing it. He/she need not express it intensely, although he/she may. Indeed, delight with a very young infant may be expressed quietly, gently, and tenderly. Even though the expression of delight may be gentle, tender, and muted, the feeling of delight is an intense one, and like all intense feelings it comes and goes. There is probably no such thing as "mild" delight. There is, however, a kind of bland, mild positive feeling—not delight—which finds frequent expression in a smiling face. It is sometimes difficult to know just how much real affect lies behind a habitually smiling face—but it is probably not delight.

Delight is situation-specific or behavior-specific, experienced and expressed in response to the baby himself/herself—in response to his/her own spontaneous expressions or reactions, or in response to his/her behavior when in interaction with his/her parent or others. As such, there is delight in the baby being himself. This delight must be distinguished from the pleasure of accomplishments, because he/she is living up to his/her expectations, doing what he/she wants him/her to do, or bringing credit to him/her in the eyes of other people. He/she may be proud that the baby is a boy, or big, or tiny, or pretty, or accelerated in development. Or a parent may take pride in his/her role as parent and in the baby as living proof that the role is truly his/hers. To

---

*Ratings of delight, sensitivity, and acceptance are derived from M. Ainsworth (undated), Maternal-care variables (available from ETS Test Collection, Educational Testing Service, Princeton, NJ, 04540).

distinguish between delight and pride is not always easy, but it can be done: delight is specific and appropriate to a situation, a response of the parent to the baby.

Sometimes delight is quite absent at first, and the only positive feeling is one of pride. Sometimes the parent is at first overwhelmed by depression and feelings of inadequacy, or, perhaps a little later, by disappointment or resentment that the baby is not what he/she expected. In such cases, delight may only gradually emerge as the baby develops, perhaps with the first social smiles, perhaps only later as the baby can take more initiative in social interaction. In any event, delight is more likely as the baby becomes more responsive. Nevertheless, in some parents it occurs from the beginning in its tender, muted form of expression.

DELIGHT

Rating

1. Delight is absent. Parent manifests no delight and little enjoyment of parenting or expresses some clear dissatisfaction with parenting. Parent may be detached or show or report mild, bland positive feelings, without the appropriate-to-situation quality of delight. Or he/she may be more or less overtly rejecting, with perhaps his/her rejection partially cloaked by his/her pride in him/herself as a parent.

2.

3. Delight is rare. Parent manifests delight or reports delight on rare occasions. More usually he/she is bland or matter-of-fact. Or, if his/her feelings are intense, they are generally prideful, but indications of true enjoyment of the infant or real satisfaction with the *experience* of parenting are missing.

4.

5. Occasional delight. Parent commonly expresses positive feeling, and occasionally manifests or reports real delight, enjoyment, or satisfaction.

6.

7. Fairly frequent delight. Delight occurs fairly frequently and appropriately in observation. Parent also reports fairly frequent delight, enjoyment, and satisfaction with parenting, along with some dissatisfaction.

8.

9. Markedly frequent delight. Parent is noted for the frequent delight he/she displays in response to baby, as well as the delight, enjoyment and satisfaction reported. He/she finds all kinds of expressions and actions of the child's as delightful. He/she is enormously interested in everything the child does, and can be delighted even with a pout or a gesture of rejection or a cry of protest. This interest is no mere curiosity or detached scientific interest. It is interest that occurs in the context generally of pleasant, uninhibited, relaxed and comfortable interaction.

INVESTMENT

Rating

1. Highly invested in parenting; parent clearly makes spending time with the child a high priority. Sees self as important to child's development. Values parenting role highly in relation to other roles.
3. Somewhat less highly invested, but time with the child still seems a high priority.
5. Somewhat uninvested in parenting; limited time is available for the child.
7. Very uninvested in parenting; other commitments (i.e., work, outside activities, etc.) take precedence over time spent with child, or even when home the parent is little involved in interacting with child.

SENSITIVITY

Rating

1. Highly insensitive. The extremely insensitive parent seems geared almost exclusively to his/her own wishes, moods, and activity. That is, parent's interventions and initiations of interaction are prompted or shaped largely by signals within herself/himself; if they mesh with baby's signals, this is often no more than coincidence. This is not to say that the parent never responds to baby's signals, for sometimes he/she does if the signals are intense enough, prolonged enough, or often enough repeated. The delay in response is in itself insensitive. Furthermore, since there is usually a disparity between the parent's own wishes and activity and baby's signals, the parent who is geared largely to his/her own signals routinely ignores or distorts the meaning of baby's behavior. Thus, when the parent responds to baby's signals, his/her response is characteristically inappropriate in kind or fragmented and incomplete.

2. Insensitive. This parent frequently fails to respond to baby's communications appropriately and/or promptly, although he/she may on some occasions show capacity for sensitivity in his/her responses to and interactions with baby. His/her insensitivity seems linked to inability to see things from baby's point of view. He/she may be too frequently preoccupied with other things and therefore inaccessible to his/her signals and communications, or he/she may misperceive his/her signals and interpret them inaccurately because of his/her own wishes or defenses, or he/she may know well enough what baby is communicating, but be disinclined to give him/her what he/she wants — because it is inconvenient or he/she is not in the mood for it, or because he/she is determined not to "spoil" him/her. He/she may delay an otherwise appropriate response to such an extent that it is no longer contingent upon his/her signal, and indeed, perhaps is no longer appropriate to his/her state, mood, or activity. Or he/she may respond with seeming appropriateness to baby's communications, but break off the transactions before baby is satisfied so that their interactions seem fragmented and incomplete, or his/her responses perfunctory, half-hearted, or impatient.

Despite such clear evidence of insensitivity, however, this parent is not as consistently or pervasively insensitive as parents with even lower ratings. Therefore, when the baby's own wishes, moods, and activity are not too deviant from the parent's wishes, moods, and household responsibilities, or when the baby is truly distressed or otherwise very forceful and compelling in his communication, this parent can modify his/her own behavior and goals and, at this time, can show some sensitivity in his/her handling of the child.

3. *Inconsistently sensitive.* Although this parent can be quite sensitive on occasion, there are some periods in which he/she is insensitive to baby's communications. Parent's inconsistent sensitivity may occur for any one of several reasons, but the outcome is that he/she seems to have lacunae in regard to his/her sensitive dealings with baby—being sensitive at some times or in respect to some aspects of his/her experience, but not in others. His/her awareness of baby may be intermittent—often fairly keen, but sometimes impervious. Or his/her perceptions of baby's behavior may be distorted in regard to one or more aspects, although it is accurate in other important aspects. He/she may be prompt and appropriate in response to his/her communications at some times and in most respects, but either inappropriate or slow at other times and in other respects. On the whole, however, he/she is more frequently sensitive than insensitive. What is striking is that a parent who can be sensitive as he/she is on so many occasions can be so insensitive on other occasions.

4. *Sensitive.* This parent also interprets baby's communications accurately, and responds to them promptly and appropriately—but with less sensitivity than parents with higher ratings. He/she may be less attuned to baby's more subtle behaviors than the highly sensitive parent. Or, perhaps because he/she is less skillful in dividing his/her attention between baby and competing demands, he/she may sometimes "miss his/her cues". Baby's clear and definite signals are, however, neither missed nor misinterpreted. This parent empathizes with baby and sees things from his point of view; his/her perceptions of his behavior are not distorted. Perhaps because his/her perception is less sensitive than that of parents with higher ratings, his/her responses are not as consistently prompt or as finely appropriate. However, although there may be occasionally little "mismatches," the parent's interventions and interactions are never seriously out of tune with baby's tempo, state, and communication.

2. *Highly sensitive.* This parent is exquisitely attuned to baby's signals, and responds to them promptly and appropriately. He/she is able to see things from baby's point of view; his/her perceptions of his/her signals and communications are not distorted by his/her own needs and defenses. He/she "reads" baby's signals and communications skillfully, and knows what the meaning is of even his/her subtle, minimal, and understated cues. He/she nearly always gives baby what he/she indicates that he/she wants, although perhaps not invariably so. When he/she feels that it is best not to comply with his/her demands—for example, when he/she is too excited, overimperious, or wants something he/she should not have—he/she is tactful in acknowledging his/her communication and in offering an acceptable alternative. He/she has "well-

rounded" interactions with baby, so that the transaction is smoothly completed and both he/she and baby feel satisfied. Finally, he/she makes his/her responses temporally contingent upon baby's signals and communications.

ACCEPTANCE

Rating

1. Highly rejecting. Parent is clearly rejecting of baby and his/her positive feelings toward him/her are frequently overwhelmed by his/her resentful, angry, rejecting feelings. This may be manifested in any one or a combination of different ways. He/she may openly voice an attitude of rejection, saying that he/she is sorry that he/she ever had him. Or he/she may somewhat less openly voice his/her rejection by implying that he/she is a great nuisance and that he/she interferes substantially in his/her life and with what he/she would like to be able to do. Or he/she may complain about baby more specifically, pointing out his/her defects and shortcomings. Even though he/she may refrain from verbalizing his/her rejection of baby, he/she may show it by a constant opposition to his/her wishes, by a generally pervasive atmosphere or irritation and scolding, by jerking him/her about with ill-concealed anger, and by joining battle with him/her whenever he/she seems to challenge his/her power. There may be positive aspects in his/her relationship with baby which suggest that he/she can enjoy baby, but these are rare and isolated in their manifestations.

3. Substantially rejecting. Parent's negative responses, veiled or open, are frequent enough to outweigh expressions of positive feelings toward baby—although he/she is neither as openly nor as strongly rejecting as a parent with lower ratings. Ways in which his/her anger or resentment toward baby may be expressed are as follows: (a) by putting him/her away from him/her when he/she does not do what he/she wants—or by deliberately ignoring him/her as retaliation—and this is not merely a matter of insensitivity, but a clear rejection of him/her; (b) by dwelling on conversation of baby's bad points and the problems he/she occasions rather than upon his/her good points, accomplishments, and the pleasure he/she yields; (c) by saying critical, uncomplimentary, nasty things to and about baby in his/her presence, even though these are "joking" (although it is difficult, these should be distinguished from "tough" comments designed to conceal strong positive feelings); (d) by a veiled irritation with baby which underlies a long-suffering, pseudo-patient compliance to his/her demands (which are perfunctory compliances and hence not satisfying) and which occasionally becomes overt in impatient, rejecting behavior; (e) marked impatience; (f) a sadistic undercurrent which is largely concealed but which comes out in little ways. Also, here one might classify the parent who shows hurt, retaliatory behavior more frequently or more strongly than the "5" or "4" parent.

5. Acceptance with strain. Parent seems chiefly positive in his/her feeling toward baby, and on occasion he/she obviously enjoys him/her; nevertheless, resentment or hurt may break through in inappropriate ways. The inappropriateness is largely a matter of the parent taking some behavior of the baby's—angry, frustrated behavior, or assertion of will, or momentary preference for other people or things — as a deep-seated, parent-directed hostility, opposition or rejection, and this leads him/her to retaliate with behavior that is essentially rejecting behavior. Or, parent may be some-what impatient and irritable with the baby at times, rejecting him/her when he/she ceases to be compliant or endearing, and yet there is enough positive interaction to preclude a lower rating. Or parent may point out either frequently or inaccurately that baby rejects him/her in that he/she seems to prefer someone else, or will not come to him/her readily. The parent, dwelling upon behavior that is interpreted as rejection, implies an undercurrent of a rejecting baby. Or parent may tease baby when he/she is upset, angry, or otherwise difficult — and the teasing, of course, aggravates the difficulty. For a rating of "5," the expressions of negative feeling must not be predominant over positive, mutually enjoyable interaction, whatever the assessment of underlying dynam-ics; if they are, the rating should be lower.

7. *Accepting.* The balance of feeling is still clearly toward the positive, accepting, loving side, and irritation and resentment are infrequent in comparison. This parent does not show as much respect for the baby as a separate, autonomous person as do parents with higher ratings, and he/she may not show as much obvious acceptance of the fact that he/she has a will of his/her own, that he/she is often interested in other people and things, and that he/she can get angry. He/she is generally patient with baby, and his/her patience seems a matter of genuine acceptance of his/her demands and inefficiencies rather than overcompliant, long-suffering, pseudo-patience. He/she seems to suppress (or repress) relatively little of his/her feeling toward baby, perhaps chiefly because there is relatively little undercurrent of negative feeling, especially toward him/her. Moreover, he/she generally accepts the limitation to his/her own autonomy presented by baby and his/her care of him/her.

9. *Complete acceptance.* Parent is highly accepting of baby and his/her behavior, even of behaviors which other parents find hurtful or irritating. He/she values the fact that the baby has a will of his/her own, even when it opposes his/hers. He/she is pleased to observe his/her interest in other people or in exploring the world, even though this may on occasion lead him/her to ignore his/her overtures. He/she even finds his/her anger worthy of respect. He/she can, on rare occasions, be irritated or frustrated by baby's behavior, but this tends to be brief — soon over and done with — and it does not occur to him/her to feel that baby himself is a worthy target upon which to focus his/her anger. He/she not only loves baby, but he/she respects him/her as an individual. At the same time he/she accepts the responsibility for caring for him/her and does not chafe against the bonds which tie him/her down temporarily and which restrict him/her from activities in which he/she would otherwise enjoy participating.

Difficulties have been encountered in rating highly defended parents who seem bland or emotionally detached and who give evidence neither of positive acceptance as defined by scale points 9 or 7, nor of the hostile components of feeling or behavior as specified by the other scale points. It seems best to rate such parents 5, despite the fact that they do not show the expressions of negative feeling specified in the definition of that scale point. It is understood that the intermediate points 4 or 6 may also be used, depending upon the tendency for either negative or positive feelings to break through the generally emotionless facade. It is further understood that there may be enough veiled rejection in a seemingly "matter of fact," emotionless parent to justify a rating of 3 as that rating point is presently defined.

APPENDIX 7b.

Time 3: Parental Involvement Rating Sheet

(Individual Interview)

Subject # _____

Time _____

Rater _____

Date _____

Delight

1	2	3	4	5	6	7	8	9
absent		rare		occasional real delight		fairly frequent		marked delight

Investment

1	2	3	4	5	6	7
highly invested		fairly invested		somewhat uninvested		very uninvested

Sensitivity

1	2	3	4	5
insensitive inappropriate		inconsistent sensitivity		highly sensitive

Acceptance

1	2	3	4	5	6	7	8	9
open resentment, rejecting		covert resentment		acceptance with strain		general acceptance		complete acceptance

Comments:

APPENDIX 8.

Time 3:
Parent-Child Interaction
Rating Scales*

(From Videotaped Parent-Child Interaction)

1. Baby's General Activity Level

This scale intends to estimate the amount of gross motor activity the baby exhibits during the play situation. At the low end of the scale the baby would have very little arm and leg movement, would not be able to help maintain sitting position, and would have trouble being able to hold his/her head erect when lying on his/her stomach. Baby at the middle point of the scale would have minimum head bobbing and be able to sit supported, helping maintain this position. A fair amount of arm and leg movement would be seen. A baby rated at this point would be considered average. At the high end of the scale vigorous arm, leg, and head movement of a constant nature would be exhibited by the baby.

1. *Very low* — Baby is very passive and exhibits minimal amounts of gross motor activity.
2. *Low* — Baby's activity is low, although baby does exhibit a small amount of gross motor activity.
3. *Intermediate* — Baby exhibits a fair amount of gross motor activity. This should be considered average.
4. *High* — Baby is an active child and exhibits gross motor activity often.
5. *Very high* — Baby is very active. Baby's gross motor activity is almost constant.

---

*Derived from M. Ainsworth (undated), Maternal care variables, and B. Egeland & E. Farber (1984), Infant-mother attachment: Factors related to its development and changes over time. *Child Development,* 55, 753-771. Copyright by The Society for Research in Child Development, Inc. Used with permission.

2. Baby's Satisfaction

This scale intends to assess the extent to which the baby is satisfied, contented, and pleased with the play situation and his/her mother's actions overall. One should attempt to balance both the intensity of the baby's positive or negative behaviors, and the relative amount of time positive and negative behavior is shown as indicators of satisfaction. The behavior of the parent should not be a factor here; that is, even if he/she does a "good job" with the child who is very discontented, he/she should be rated as very discontented. This is a rating of the baby, not of an aspect of interaction per se.

1. *Extremely discontented* — Baby shows extreme dissatisfaction, irritability, and crying. Strong intensity dissatisfaction is seen, and discontent is by far the predominant state.

3. *Somewhat discontented* — Dissatisfaction dominates the baby's reaction (though some positive reaction might be seen).

5. *Baby reacts negatively and positively* to some aspects of the situation in about equal proportion or is basically neutral and unresponsive.

7. *Contented* — Baby is mostly satisfied and displays a generally positive (in intensity or time) reaction to the situation (though some negative reaction might be seen).

9. *Very contented* — Baby is generally very pleased and happy in the situation, displaying strong, positive reactions as well as a by far predominantly positive state.

3. Child's State

A. *Baby's Predominant State* — This scale intends to estimate the baby's state in the play situation.

B. *Baby's Best State* — This scale intends to assess the best state the baby achieved during the play situation.

1. Alert look, but doesn't seem to focus attention on source of stimulation and/or on parent.

2. Alert look, and seems to focus attention on source of stimulation and/or parent.

3. Fussy.

4. Crying.

4. Child's Attention

One important variable in the quality of the interaction in the case of working and playing is due to his/her attention — how easily the parent can gain his/her attention and encourage him to focus it on him/her or an object, and how well he/she can maintain his/her attention on the object or his/her parent in the face of surrounding distractions. While the actions of the parent are necessarily involved here, insofar as possible, one should attempt to estimate the baby's attention independent of the parent's behavior. The scale is constructed so that a baby who seems to be dazed and unarousable is on the low end of the scale, and on the opposite end are babies who are distractible and unable to maintain their attention for more than a brief moment.

Thus, a baby who is able to balance the needs to maintain and to shift attention well would receive a 5 rating.

1. *Unarousable* — The baby seems dazed and unaccessible to all but intense physical stimulation or manipulation.
3. *Somewhat unarousable* — The baby's attention is difficult to gain and manipulate, but strong, clear efforts are able to arouse and direct baby's attention.
5. *Balanced, adequate attention* — The baby's attention is neither difficult to gain nor easily lost, and he/she is consequently receptive to the parent's actions and the possibilities of extending play with a single object.
7. *Somewhat distracted* — The baby's attention shifts rapidly from one stimulus to another, and it is thus difficult, though possible with persistence and care, to engage the baby in an extended interaction.
9. *Distracted* — The baby's attention shifts extremely rapidly at the slightest external stimulation or for no apparent reason. It is thus not possible to engage him in an extended interaction or maintain his/her focus on one object for more than a moment.

5. Parent's Supportiveness

This scale intends to estimate the parent's use of verbal and gestural means to involve the child in doing something or continuing an action. This refers to remarks and expressions of approval, solicitation, etc. that are directed towards some action of the baby or are in response to his/her action in a general way. The scale moves from unsupportiveness at the lower end, due either to distancing from the child or an overbearing intensity, to an optimally supportive style on the other extreme. If a rating less than 5 is given, please note if the parent's tendency is toward aloofness or overbearingness or both.

1. Parent remains totally aloof from the child, psychologically and/or physically, or is extremely overbearing, physically interfering and dominant. This is a constant and dominant feature of their interaction.
3. Parent is either generally removed or distanced from his/her child or often interferes and dominates so that child's initiative is thwarted. These are neither as vigorous nor constant as in a lower ratings.
5. Parent shows some tendencies towards distancing or overbearingness, but is basically neutral or somewhat supportive of the child.
7. Parent is generally and actively supportive of the child in verbal and gestural ways, though some small bit of unsupportive behavior or neutral behavior is seen.
9. Parent is continuously supportive of the child.

6. Parent's Activity Level

1. Distant.
3. Low passive interaction — Parent exhibits very little physical or verbal activity in the play situation.

5. Intermediate level of activity—In the play situation the parent exhibits a fair amount of activity that is high in intensity, interspersed with periods of low activity.

7. High.

9. Extremely high—Parent exhibits constant activity, most of which is intense in tone and movement.

7. Parent's Attitude Towards Playing with the Child

Since this is a play situation, some of the characteristics of a playful attitude might be seen here, but these will be observed in varying degrees in different parents. It is not only this playfulness of the parent which is intended here, but his/her ENJOYMENT of playing with the baby. Thus, interaction with the baby is an important element. This is not, however, intended to measure baby's enjoyment or activity or the synchrony of the interaction, but rather the PARENT'S FEELING ABOUT playing with the child. His/her attitude might range from active dislike, with active negative feelings being expressed towards the situation or the child, to neutrality in which he/she carries out the experimenter's instructions but with no enthusiasm or spontaneous motivation of his/her own, to active enjoyment in which the structure of the situation is secondary to the warm, vigorous, spontaneous pleasing of interaction with the child in play.

1. *Strong, active dislike*, e.g., hitting the child, roughly forcing his/her actions, or yelling at the child.

3. *Slight, passive dislike*, e.g., mild disparaging remarks, or a moping through the time with a passive resistance and a desire to quickly terminate the interaction.

5. *Bland, emotionless neutrality*, e.g., a bland, affectless neutrality might be encountered in which no feelings are expressed and no passive resistance to playing is seen, but neither is enjoyment or involvement in the interaction with the child.

7. *Slight tender enjoyment*, e.g., some encouragement to or tenderness toward the child observed, smiling in response to the interaction, or a moderate effort to maintain contact with the child.

9. *Much active enjoyment*, e.g., a strong, ongoing, spontaneous, effusive or obviously pleasurable involvement with the child, with encouragement, laughing, warmth or tenderness observed in the reciprocal, sharing nature of the play.

8. Parent's Inventiveness—Repertoire of Behaviors

This scale estimates the range of stimulation the parent is able to provide his/her baby: the number of different approaches and types of interactions, his/her ability to find different things to interest the child, different ways of using the toys, combining the toys and inventing games with or without toys. It refers to invention directed toward and effective in maintaining baby's involvement in the situation and not to uses pleasing to adults but not to babies, i.e., not merely to the number of different, random behaviors, but to the numbered behaviors grouped to and directed towards the baby.

1. *Very small repertoire*—Parent is able to do almost nothing with his/her baby, seems at a loss for ideas, stumbles around, is unsure of what to do. His/her actions are simple, stereotyped, and repetitive.

3. *Small repertoire* — Parent does find a few ways to engage the child in the course of the situation, but these are of limited number and tend to be repeated frequently, possibly with long periods of inactivity. He/she uses the toys in some of the standard ways, but does not seem to use other possibilities with toys or free play.

5. *Medium repertoire* — Parent has available to him/her the normal playing behaviors, shows ability to use the standard means of playing with the toys, and the usual means of free play.

7. *Large repertoire* — Parent has available to him/her and shows ability to use all the usual playing behaviors, but in addition, is able to find a few uses which are especially appropriate to the situation and his/her baby's momentary needs.

9. *Very large repertoire* — Parent is consistently finding new ways to use the toys and his/her own actions to play with the baby. He/she shows both standard uses of the toys and many unusual but appropriate uses and continually is able to change his/her behavior in response to the baby's needs and state.

9. Reciprocal Play

This scale attempts to assess the quality of reciprocal play between parent and infant, disregarding quality if the interaction meets the minimum standards for reciprocal play. The first aspect of these standards is mutual attention to the game-like interaction which is the focus of the ongoing play. Ongoing means an interaction of at least a few seconds in which both the parent and child have taken some active part. Secondly, some alternation or response is necessary. This does not necessarily mean an object manipulation, since a look, a gasp, or a verbalization can each be an adequate response which will continue the play. A negative test can be applied here — that is, if the behavior (from brightening look to grabbing, etc.) had not been emitted, would the interaction have continued; if it would not have, a response sufficient to qualify as alternating has occurred. Finally, contingency must be seen — that is, the behavior emitted must be appropriate to the situation and to the immediately preceding response and must be temporally appropriate.

1. None.
2. Few brief, unsuccessful attempts by one partner to engage in reciprocal play.
3. A few brief, unsustained episodes of reciprocal play.
4. One instance of reciprocal play that perpetuates itself.
5. A few instances of reciprocal play that perpetuate themselves.
6. Less than 25 percent of reciprocal play.
7. Quite a bit of reciprocal play (25-50 percent).
8. Reciprocal play predominates during the episode (50-75 percent).
9. Nearly constant reciprocal play (over 75 percent).

10. Parent's Appropriateness of Play

1. *Very inappropriate play* — Parent's play with baby is inappropriate because: (a) it is controlling, teasing or even tormenting; (b) it is grossly overstimulating; (c) it is very badly geared to baby's developmental level, being either mechanical,

simple and boring, or far beyond baby's capacities for response; or (d) because it is obviously for parent's own gratification rather than for baby's pleasure.

3. *Inappropriate play*—Parent's play with baby is inappropriate because: (a) it is mechanical and unspontaneous; (b) it is an attempt to distract or instruct baby rather than to give him/her enjoyment; or (c) it has some of the features of being overstimulating, controlling, teasing, or overextending without warranting a lower rating.

5. *Moderately appropriate play*—Parents play with baby sometimes fairly spontaneously, sometimes mechanically. But either he/she lacks the capacity for delighted interaction that is implied by higher ratings, or he/she intersperses inappropriate play characteristic of lower ratings (occasionally), or a combination of both.

7. *Appropriate play*—When parent plays with baby he/she seems to have baby's enjoyment as his/her chief purpose, and at the same time to enjoy it himself. He/she has some spontaneity and flexibility. He has considerable ability to adapt his/her play to baby's mood and level of development. He/she may overstimulate occasionally, but he/she usually knows when it is time to stop play, or at least to reduce its level of intensity.

9. *Very appropriate play*—Parent plays with baby spontaneously and delightedly. His/her play is sensitively appropriate to baby's mood and level of development. He/she constantly gears his/her play actions to cues given by baby's behavior, and, indeed, play is so interwoven with his/her routine care and other interactions with baby that it is can scarcely be distinguished from it.

11. Parental Sensitivity

1. *Highly insensitive*—The extremely insensitive parent seems geared almost exclusively to his/her own wishes, moods, and activity. Thus, parent's interventions and initiations of interactions are prompted or shaped largely by signals within herself/himself; if they mesh with baby's signals, this is often no more than coincidence. This is not to say that the parent never responds to baby's signals, for sometimes he/she does if the signals are intense enough, prolonged enough, or often enough repeated. The delay in response is in itself insensitive. Furthermore, there is usually a disparity between parents own wishes and activity and baby's signals. The parent is geared largely to his/her own signals, routinely ignoring or distorting the meaning of baby's behavior. Thus, when parent responds to baby's signals, the response is characteristically inappropriate in kind or fragmented and incomplete.

3. *Insensitive*—This parent frequently fails to respond to baby's communications appropriately and/or promptly, although he/she may on some occasions show capacity for sensitivity in responses to and interactions with baby. The insensitivity seems linked to inability to see things from baby's point of view. He/she may be preoccupied too frequently with other things and therefore inaccessible to baby's signals and communications, or he/she may misperceive baby's signals and interpret them inaccurately because of his/her own wishes or defenses, or he/she may know well enough what baby is communicating but be disinclined to give baby what he/she wants—whether because it is inconvenient or he/she is not in the mood for it, or because he/she is determined not to

"spoil" baby. An otherwise appropriate response may be delayed to such an extent that it is no longer contingent upon baby's signal, and indeed perhaps is no longer appropriate to baby's state, mood, or activity. Or the parent may respond with seeming appropriateness to baby's communications but break off the transactions before baby is satisfied so that their interactions seem fragmented and incomplete or the responses perfunctory, half-hearted, or impatient.

Despite such clear evidence of insensitivity, however, this parent is not as consistently or pervasively insensitive as parents with even lower ratings. Therefore, when the baby's own wishes, moods, and activity are not too deviant from the parent's wishes, moods, and household responsibilities, or when the baby is truly distressed or otherwise very forceful and compelling in his/her communication, this parent can modify his/her own behavior and goals and, at this time, can show some sensitivity in the handling of the child.

5. *Inconsistently sensitive* — Although this parent can be quite sensitive on occasion, there are some periods in which he/she is insensitive to baby's communications. Parent's inconsistent sensitivity may occur for any one of several reasons, but the outcome is that he/she seems to have lacunae in regard to his/her sensitive dealing with baby — being sensitive at some times or in respect to some aspects of his/her experience, but not in others. The awareness of baby may be intermittent — often fairly keen, but sometimes impervious. Or the perception of baby's behavior may be distorted in regard to one or two aspects although it is accurate in other important aspects. He/she may be prompt and appropriate in response to baby's communications at some times and in some respects, but either inappropriate or slow at other times and in other respects. On the whole, however, he/she is more frequently sensitive than insensitive. What is striking is that a parent who can be as sensitive on so many occasions can be so insensitive on other occasions.

7. *Sensitive* — This parent also interprets baby's communications accurately, and responds to them promptly and appropriately, but with less sensitivity than parents with higher ratings. He/she may be less attuned to baby's more subtle behaviors than the highly sensitive parent. Or, perhaps because this parent is less skillful in dividing the attention between baby and competing demands, he/she may sometimes "miss the cues." Baby's clear and definite signals are, however, neither missed nor misinterpreted. This parent emphathizes with baby and sees things from his/her point of view; the perceptions of his/her behavior are not distorted. Perhaps because the perception is less sensitive than that of parents with higher ratings, the responses are not as consistently prompt or as finely appropriate — but although there may be occasional little "mismatches," parent's interventions and interactions are never seriously out of tune with baby's tempo, state, and communications.

9. *Highly sensitive* — This parent is exquisitely attuned to baby's signals, and responds to them promptly and appropriately. He/she is able to see things from baby's point of view; perceptions of his/her signals and communications are not distorted by his/her own needs and defenses. He/she "reads" baby's signals and communications skillfully, and knows what the meaning is of even his/her subtle, minimal, and understated cues. He/she nearly always gives baby what he/she indicates he/she wants, although perhaps not invariably so. When he/she feels that it is best not to comply with his/her demands — for example,

when baby is too excited, overimperious, or wants something he/she should not have — parent is tactful in acknowledging his/her communication and in offering an acceptable alternative. He/she has "well-rounded" interactions with baby, so that the transaction is smoothly completed and both parent and baby feel satisfied. Finally, he/she makes responses temporally contingent upon baby's signals and communications.

12. Animation of Parent's Facial and Vocal Expression

1. Parent generally presents a flat, blank, expressionless face and voice.
2. Parent generally presents a flat, blank, expressionless face and voice, with some moments of animation, though rare. May or may not seem ill-timed.
3. Parent presents flat, blank, expressionless face and voice about half the time, with some animation, though not full-blown the rest of the time and/or not entirely appropriate.
4. Parent has appropriate animation all of the time, though somewhat dampened.
5. Parent is very animated, provides sparkling eyes, expressive face and voice to child in an appropriate manner.

13. Overall Affective Tone

1. Very positive.
2. Slightly positive.
3. Negative and positive affect in about equal proportion or is predominantly neutral.
4. Slightly negative.
5. Very negative.

GLOBAL RATINGS T3

\# _____ Mother   Father   _____ Rater _____ Date

1. Child's Activity Level
   1 2 3 4 5

2. Child's Satisfaction
   1 2 3 4 5 6 7 8 9

3A. Child's State
   1 2 3 4

3B. Best State Achieved
   1 2 3 4

4. Child's Attention
   1 2 3 4 5 6 7 8 9

5. Parent's Supportiveness
   1 2 3 4 5 6 7 8 9

6. Parent's Activity Level
   1 2 3 4 5 6 7 8 9

7. Parent's Attitude to Play
   1 2 3 4 5 6 7 8 9

8. Parent's Inventiveness
   1 2 3 4 5 6 7 8 9

9. Reciprocal Play
   1 2 3 4 5 6 7 8 9

10. Parent's Appropriateness of Play
    1 2 3 4 5 6 7 8 9

11. Parental Sensitivity
    1 2 3 4 5 6 7 8 9

12. Animation of Parent
    1 2 3 4 5

13. Overall Affective Tone
    1 2 3 4 5

Notes:

APPENDIX 9.

Time 4:
Triadic Competence
Rating Scales

(From M-F-C Videotaped Interaction)

1. ACTIVITY PATTERN

Family Number _____

Interaction Observed _____

Rater _____ Date _____

This is a global scale designed to describe the *predominant form of interaction observed between parents and child.* The participants' behavior may fall in several different categories over the course of the total observation. For example, at times all three may be involved jointly, followed by a period in which one parent withdraws, interspersed with brief episodes of parental competition for the child's attention. Select the *one category* that most clearly describes the predominant form of interaction after observing the entire videotape.

1. Parents and child jointly involved in play. Both parents are involved with child and with each other. All three individuals are engaged in activity together. There is a clear triadic element or tone to the interaction.

2. Parents take turns individually playing with the child; some interaction between parents. Parents take turns interacting with the child; noninteracting parent remains an interested spectator. Parents relate somewhat to each other through conversation, gaze, or shared affect, but they do not actively play together with the child. The parents are not competing with or intruding upon each other, but the style of interaction is essentially alternating dyads with an involved spectator.

3. *Parents are involved with the child individually, but do not interact with each other.* This is similar to category number 2, except there is little or no parent-to-parent interaction.

4. *Parents are involved with the child individually and compete for the child's attention and involvement.* There are frequent instances in which the play of one parent with the child is interrupted by the efforts of the other parent to engage the child. Parents are involved sequentially in attempts to compete with or intrude upon the other's involvement with the child; these efforts may or may not succeed.

5. *One parent is involved with the child almost exclusively, while the other parent essentially withdraws from the interaction.* One parent is uninvolved for most of the interaction period. He or she may make occasional efforts to be involved, but these appear perfunctory or are quickly resisted by the other parent or the child. In scoring this form of interaction, *note which parent is involved and which is uninvolved:* MI, MU, FI, FU.

6. *Parents are involved with each other separate from the child.* The parents' involvement with each other, either positive or negative, is primarily separate from or excludes the child. There may be periodic efforts by one or both parents to engage the child, but these tend to be short-lived.

2. TRIADIC AFFECT SCALES

Family Number _____

Interaction Observed _____

Rater _____ Date _____

In using the following three subscales, there will be clear variation in the qualities measured from moment to moment. Please, however, select the rating that best fits the entire period.

A. *Affective Quality*

1. Distinctly pleasurable
2. Neutral, joyless, or perfunctory, as for example, moments of anger or other negative affect compensated for through formal or stilted "niceness"; or mixtures of mildly negative and mildly pleasurable affect
3. Predominantly negative

B. *Affective Intensity:* May be positive, negative, or mixed

   1. High
   2. Moderate
   3. Low

C. *Affective Involvement*

   1. All 3 participants share affect(s)
   2. 2 of 3 participants share affect(s) at one time
   3. Each participant involved in his or her own affect with little or no affect(s) shared

References

Ainsworth, M. (undated) Maternal-care variables. (Available from ETS Test Collection, Educational Testing Service, Princeton, NJ 0854).

Ainsworth, M., Blehar, M., Waters, E., & Wall, S. (1978). *Patterns of Attachment*. New Jersey: Erlbaum.

Anthony, E. J. (1970). The impact of mental and physical illness on family life. *American Journal of Psychiatry, 127*(2), 56-64.

Barnhill, L. R., & Longo, D. (1978). Fixation and regression in the family life cycle. *Family Process, 17*, 469-478.

Bateson, G. (1978). *Mind and nature*. New York: E. P. Dutton.

Beavers, W. R. (1977). *Psychotherapy and growth: A family systems perspective*. New York: Brunner/Mazel.

Beck, A. T., Ward, C. H., Mendelson, M., Mock, J., & Erbaugh, J. (1961). An inventory for measuring depression. *Archives of General Psychiatry, 4*, 53-64.

Belsky, J., & Pensky, E. (in press). Developmental history, personality, and family relationships: Toward an emergent family system. In R. Hinde & J. Stevenson-Hinde (Eds.), *Towards understanding families*. London: Cambridge Press.

Belsky, J., Spainer, G. B., & Rovine, M. (1983). Stability and change in marriage across the transition to parenthood. *Journal of Marriage and the Family, 45*, 567-577.

Benedek, T. (1959). Parenthood as a developmental phase. *Journal of American Psychoanalytic Association, 7*, 389-417.

Berman, E. M., & Lief, H. I. (1975). Marital therapy from a psychiatric perspective: An overview. *American Journal of Psychiatry, 132*(6), 583-592.

Boles, A. J. (1983). Marital satisfaction during the transition to parenthood. Presented at the American Psychological Association Meeting, Anaheim, California.

Boszormenyi-Nagy, I. (1965). A theory of relationships: Experience and transaction. In I. Boszormenyi-Nagy, & J. L. Framo (Eds.), *Intensive family therapy: Theoretical and practical aspects*. New York: Harper & Row, 33-86.

Bowen, M. (1960). A family concept of schizophrenia. In D. D. Jackson (Ed.), *The etiology of schizophrenia*. New York: Basic Books, 346-372.

Bowen, M. (1965). Family psychotherapy with schizophrenia in the hospital and in private practice. In I. Boszormenyi-Nagy & J. L. Framo (Eds.), *Intensive family therapy: Theoretical and practical aspects*. New York: Hoeber Medical Division, Harper & Row, 213-243.

Bowen, M. (1986). On the differentiation of self. In M. Bowen, (Ed.), *Family therapy in clinical practice*. Northvale, New Jersey: Jason Aronson.

Brodman, K., Erdmann, A., & Wolff, H. (1949). *Cornell Medical Index*. (Available from Cornell University Medical College, New York).

Brooks, J. (1981). Social maturity in middle-life and its developmental antecedents. In D. Eichorn, J. Clausen, N. Haan, M. Honzik, and P. Mussen (Eds.), *Present and past in middle life*. New York: Academic Press, 243-265.

Brown, G. W., & Harris, T. (1978). *Social origins of depression*. New York: The Free Press.

Bruner, J. (1986). *Actual minds, possible worlds*. Cambridge, MA: Harvard University Press.

Caldwell, B. M., & Bradley, R. H. (1987). *HOME observation for measurement of the environment*. Homewood, IL: Dorsey Press.

Carter, E. A., & McGoldrick, M. (1980). The family life cycle and family therapy: An overview. In E. A. Carter & M. McGoldrick (Eds.), *The family life cycle: A framework for family therapy*. New York: Gardner Press, 3-20.

Cohler, B. J., & Boxer, A. M. (1984). Middle adulthood: Settling into the world—person, time, and context. In D. Offer & M. Sabshin (Eds.), *Normality and the life cycle: A critical integration*. New York: Basic Books, 145-203.

Combrinck-Graham, L. (1985). A developmental model for family systems. *Family Process, 24,* 139-150.

Cowan, C. P., & Cowan, P. A. (1981). Conflicts for partners becoming parents: Implications for the couple relationship. Paper presented at the American Psychological Association Symposium on Research on Families, Los Angeles.

Cowan, C. P., & Cowan, P. A. (1985a). Parents' work patterns, marital and parent-child relationships, and early child development. Paper presented at the Meetings of the Society for Research in Child Development, Toronto.

Cowan, C. P., Cowan, P. A., Coie, L., & Coie, J. D. (1978). Becoming a family: The impact of a first child's birth on the couples' relationship. In W. Miller & E. Newman (Eds.), *The first child and family formation*. Chapel Hill: Carolina Population Center, 296-324.

Cowan, C. P., Cowan, P. A., Heming, G., Garrett, E., Coysh, W. S., Curtis-Boles, H., & Boles, A. J., III (1985). Transitions to parenthood: His, hers, and theirs, *Journal of Family Issues,* 6(4), 451-481.

Cowan, P. A., & Ball, L. J. (1981). The impact of the first child on couple communication. Paper presented at the American Psychological Association Meeting, Los Angeles.

Cowan, P. A., & Cowan, C. P. (1983). Quality of couple relationships and parenting stress in beginning families. Paper presented at the Meetings for the Society of Research in Child Development, Detroit.

Cowan, P. A., & Cowan, C. P. (1985b). Pregnancy, parenthood, and children at three. Paper presented at the Meetings of the Society for Research in Child Development, Toronto.

Cox, M. J. (1985). Progress and continued challenges in understanding the transition to parenthood. *Journal of Family Issues, 6*(4), 395-408.

Cox, M. J., Owen, M. T., Lewis, J. M., Riedel, C., Scalf-McIver, L., & Suster, A. (1985). Intergenerational influences on the parent-infant relationship in the transition to parenthood. *Journal of Family Issues, 6*(4), 543-564.

Cuber, J. F., & Harroff, P. B. (1965). *The significant Americans: A study of sexual behavior among the affluent.* New York: Appleton-Century.

Dell, P., & Goolishian, G. (1979). Order through fluctuation: An evolutionary epistemology for human systems. Presented at the Annual Scientific Meeting of the A. K. Rice Institute, Houston, Texas.

Dyer, E. D. (1963). Parenthood as crisis: A re-study. *Marriage and Family Living, 25,* 196-201.

Egeland, B., & Farber, E. (1984). Infant-mother attachment: Factors related to its development and changes over time. *Child Development, 55,* 753-771.

Elder, G., Caspi, A., & Downey, G. (1986). Problem behavior and family relationships: Life course and intergenerational themes. In A. Sorensen, F. Weinert, & L. Sherrod (Eds.), *Human development and the life course: Multidisciplinary perspectives.* Hillsdale, NJ: Erlbaum Associates, 293-340.

Engel, G. L. (1980). The clinical application of the biopsychosocial model. *The American Journal of Psychiatry, 137*(5), 535-544.

Erikson, E. H. (1963). *Childhood and society, Second edition.* New York: W. W. Norton.

Feldman, L. B. (1979). Marital conflict and marital intimacy: An integrative psychodynamic-behavioral-systemic model. *Family Process, 18*(1), 69-78.

Foerster, H. von (1984). On constructing a reality. In P. Watzlawick (Ed.), *The invented reality: How do we know what we believe we know? (Contributions to constructivism).* New York: W. W. Norton & Company, 41-68.

Framo, J. L. (1976). Family of origin as a therapeutic resource for adults in marital and family therapy: You can and should go home again. *Family Process, 15*(2), 193-210.

Gallagher, J. (Undated). *Role Survey.* Unpublished manuscript. Chapel Hill, NC: Frank Porter Graham Child Development Center.

Glasserfeld, E. von (1984). An introduction to radical constructivism. In P. Watzlawick (Ed.), *The invented reality: How do we know what we believe we know? (Contributions to constructivism).* New York: W. W. Norton & Company, 17-40.

Goodman, N. (1984). *Of mind and other matters.* Cambridge, MA: Harvard University Press.

Goodrich, W. (1968). Toward a taxonomy of marrige. In J. Marmor (Ed.), *Modern psychoanalysis.* New York: Basic Books, 407-423.

Goodrich, W. (1985). Personal communication.

Gossett, J. T., Barnhart, F. D., Lewis, J. M., & Phillips, V. A. (1977). Follow-up of adolescents treated in a psychiatric hospital: Predictors of outcome. *Archives of General Psychiatry, 34,* 1037-1042.

Gossett, J. T., Lewis, J. M., & Barnhart, F. D. (1983). *To find a way: The outcome of hospital treatment of disturbed adolescents.* New York: Brunner/Mazel.

Gossett, J. T., Meeks, J. E., Barnhart, F. D., & Phillips, V. A. (1976). Follow-up of adolescents treated in a psychiatric hospital: The onset of symptomatology scale. *Adolescence, 11,* 195-211.

Gough, H. G. (1975). *Manual for the California Psychological Inventory.* Palo Alto, CA: Consulting Psychologists Press.

Gough, H. G., & Heilbrun, A. B. (1965). The adjective checklist. Palo Alto, CA: Consulting Psychologists Press.

Grossman, F. K., Eichler, L. S., Winickoff, S. A., Anzalone, M. K., Gofseyeff, M. H., & Sargent, S. P. (1980). Pregnancy, birth, and parenthood. San Francisco: Jossey-Bass.

Gurman, A. S. (1983). Research and clinical exchange. The American Journal of Family Therapy, 11(1), 67-72.

Hafner, R. J. (1986). Marriage and mental illness: A sex-role perspective. New York: Guilford Press.

Haley, J. (1980). Leaving home: The therapy of disturbed young people. New York: McGraw-Hill.

Haley, J. (1981). Reflections on therapy and other essays. Washington, DC: The Family Therapy Institute.

Havens, L. L. (1973). Approaches to the mind: Movement of the psychiatric schools from sects toward science. Boston: Little, Brown & Co.

Heming, G. (1981). Early identification of couples at risk. Paper presented at the American Psychological Association Meeting, Los Angeles.

Hill, R. (1949). Families under stress. New York: Harper.

Hill, R. & Mattessich, P. (1979). Family development theory and life span development. Life Span Development and Behavior, 2, 161-204.

Hobbs, D. F. (1965). Parenthood as crisis: A third study. Journal of Marriage and the Family, 27, 367-372.

Hobbs, D. F. (1968). Transition to parenthood: A replication and extension. Journal of Marriage and the Family, 30, 413-417.

Hobbs, D. F., & Cole, S. P. (1976). Transition to parenthood: A decade replication. Journal of Marriage and the Family, 38(4), 723-731.

Hobbs, D. F., & Wimbish, J. M. (1977). Transition to parenthood by black couples. Journal of Marriage and the Family, 39(4), 677-689.

Hock, E., Christman, K., & Hock, M. (1980). Factors associated with decisions about return to work in mothers of infants. Developmental Psychology, 16 (5), 535-536.

Hoffman, L. (1980). The family life cycle and discontinuous change. In E. A. Carter & M. McGoldrick (Eds.), The family life cycle: A framework for family therapy. New York: Gardner Press, 53-68.

Hoffman, L. (1981). Foundations of family therapy: A conceptual framework for systems change. New York: Basic Books.

Hollingshead, A. B. (1975). Four-factor index of social status. Available from author: P.O. Box 1965, Yale Station, New Haven, Connecticut 06520.

Jacoby, A. P. (1969). Transition to parenthood: A reassessment. Journal of Marriage and the Family, 31, 720-727.

Kantor, D., & Lehr, W. (1975). Inside the family: Toward a theory of family process. San Francisco: Jossey-Bass.

Kaplan, A. G. (1984). The "self-in-relation": Implications for depression in women. Work in Progress. Wellesley, MA: Wellesley College Stone Center for Developmental Services and Studies.

Kaplan, A., Klein, R., & Gleason, N. (1985). Women's self development in late adolescence. Work in Progress, Wellesley, MA: Wellesley College Stone Center for Developmental Services and Studies.

Karpel, M. (1976). Individuation: From fusion to dialogue. Family Process, 15(1), 65-82.

LeMasters, E. E. (1957). Parenthood as crisis. *Marriage and Family Living, 19,* 352-355.

Levinson, D. J., with Darrow, C. N., Klein, E. B., Levinson, M. H., & McKee, B. (1978). *The seasons of a man's life.* New York: Alfred A. Knopf.

Lewis, J. M. (1986). Family structure and stress. *Family Process, 25,* 235-247.

Lewis, J. M. (1988). Theoretical approaches to family of origin influences on marital object choice. Unpublished manuscript.

Lewis, J. M., Beavers, W. R., Gossett, J. T., & Phillips, V. A. (1976). *No single thread: Psychological health in family systems.* New York: Brunner/Mazel.

Lewis, J. M., Gossett, J. T., & Phillips, V. A. (1971). A research study of healthy families. *Journal of the National Association of Private Psychiatric Hospitals, 3*(1), 20-23.

Lewis, J. M., & Looney, J. G. (1983). *The long struggle: Well-functioning working-class black families.* New York: Brunner/Mazel.

Lidz, T., Cornelison, A. R., Fleck, S., & Terry D. (1957). The intrafamilial environment of schizophrenic patients: II. Marital schism and marital skew. *American Journal of Psychiatry, 114,* 241-248.

Lidz, T., & Fleck, S. (1965). *Schizophrenia and the family.* New York: International Universities Press.

Locke, H. J., & Wallace, K. M. (1959). Short marital adjustment and prediction tests: Their reliability and validity. *Marriage and Family Living, 21,* 251-255.

Loevinger, J., & Wessler, R. (1970). *Measuring ego development, Vol. 1.* San Francisco: Jossey Bass.

Loevinger, J., Wessler, R., & Redmore, C. (1970). *Measuring ego development, Vol. 2.* San Francisco: Jossey Bass.

Magrabi, F. M., & Marshall, W. H. (1965). Family developmental tasks: A research model. *Journal of Marriage and the Family,* 454-461.

Main, M., & Weston, D. R. (1981). The quality of the toddler's relationship to mother and to father: Related to conflict behavior and the readiness to establish new relationships. *Child Development, 52*(3), 932-940.

Margolis, L. (Undated). *Social Network Survey.* Unpublished manuscript. Department of Pediatrics, University of Chicago Medical School.

Martin, P. A. (1976). *A marital therapy manual.* New York: Brunner/Mazel.

Maruyama, M. (1968). The second cybernetics: Deviation-amplifying mutual causal processes. In W. Buckley (Ed.), *Modern systems research for the behavioral scientist.* Chicago: Aldine.

McCubbin, H. I., & Patterson, J. M. (1983). *Family stress and adaptation to crises: A double ABCX model of family behavior.* Beverly Hills: Sage Publications.

McDermott, J. F., Jr., Robillard, A. B., Char, W. F., Hsu, J., Tseng, W., & Ashton, G. C. (1983). Reexamining the concept of adolescence: Differences between adolescent boys and girls in the context of their families. *American Journal of Psychiatry, 140*(10), 1319-1322.

Meissner, W. W. (1978). The conceptualization of marriage and family dynamics from a psychoanalytic perspective. In T. J. Paolino, Jr., & B. S. McCrady (Eds.), *Marriage and marital therapy: Psychoanalytic, behavioral and systems theory perspectives.* New York: Brunner/Mazel, 25-88.

Meyerowitz, J. H., & Feldman, H. (1966). Transition to parenthood. *Psychiatric Research Reports, 20,* 78-84.

Miller, J. G. (1984). The development of women's sense of self. *Work in Progress.* Wellesley: MA. Wellesley College, Stone Center for Developmental Services and Studies.

Minuchin, P. (1985). Families and individual development: Provocations from the field of family therapy. *Child Development, 56,* 289-302.

Minuchin, S., Baker, L., Rosman, B. L., Liebman, R., Milman, L., & Todd, T. C. (1975). A conceptual model of psychosomatic illness in children. *Archives of General Psychiatry, 32*(8), 1031-1038.

Neugarten, B. L. (1979). Time, age, and the life cycle. *The American Journal of Psychiatry, 136*(7), 886-894.

Oldham, D. G. (1978). Adolescent turmoil: A myth revisited. In S. C. Feinstein & P. L. Giovacchine (Eds.), *Adolescent psychiatry, Vol. VI, Developmental and clinical studies.* Chicago: University of Chicago Press, 267-279.

Paulhus, D., & Christie, R. (1981). Spheres of control: An interactionist approach to assessment of perceived control. In H. M. Lefcourt (Ed.), *Research with the locus of control construct, Vol. 1,* New York: Academic Press, 161-188.

Prigogine, I. (1969). Structure, dissipation and life. In *Theoretical physics and biology.* Amsterdam, Holland: North Holland Publishing Company.

Quinton, D., & Rutter, M. (1985). Parenting behavior of mothers raised "in care." In A. Nicol (Ed.), *Longitudinal studies in child psychology and psychiatry.* London: Wiley, 157-210.

Quinton, D., Rutter, M., & Liddle, C. (1984). Institutional rearing, parenting difficulties and marital support. *Psychological Medicine, 14,* 107-124.

Rapoport, R. (1963). Normal crisis, family structure and mental health. *Family Process, 2,* 68-80.

Raush, H. L., Barry, W. A., Hertel, R. K., Swain, M. A. (1974). *Communication conflict and marriage.* San Francisco: Jossey Bass.

Reiss, D. (1981). *The family's construction of reality.* Cambridge, MA: Harvard University Press.

Reiss, D., Gonzalez, S., & Kramer, N. (1986). Family process, chronic illness, and death. *Archives of General Psychiatry, 43*(8), 795-804.

Rogler, L. H., & Hollingshead, A. B. (1965). *Trapped: Families and schizophrenia.* New York: John Wiley & Sons.

Rounsaville, B. J., Weissman, M. M., Prusoff, B. A., & Herceg-Baron, R. L. (1979). Marital disputes and treatment outcome in depressed women. *Comprehensive Psychiatry, 20*(5), 483-490.

Roy, A. (1981). Vulnerability factors and depression in men. *British Journal of Psychiatry, 138,* 75-77.

Russell, C. S. (1974). Transition to parenthood: Problems and gratifications. *Journal of Marriage and the Family, 36*(2), 294-302.

Rutter, M. (1982). Protective factors in children's responses to stress on disadvantage. In M. W. Kent & J. E. Rolf (Eds.), *Primary prevention of psychopathology, Vol. 3. Promoting social competence and coping in children.* Hanover, NH: University Press of New England, 49-74.

Rutter, M., & Quinton, C. (1984). Long-term follow-up of women institutionalized in childhood: Factors promoting good functioning in adult life. *British Journal of Developmental Psychology, 2,* 191-204.

Sagan, L. A. (March-April, 1988). Family ties: The real reason people are living longer. *The Sciences.*

Sampson, H. Messinger, S. L., & Towne, R. D. (1964). *Schizophrenic women: Studies in marital crisis.* New York: Atherton Press.

Sarason, I. G., Johnson, J. H., & Siegel, J. M. (1978). Assessing the impact of life changes: Development of the life experiences survey. *Journal of Consulting and Clinical Psychology, 46*(5), 932-946.

Sharpe, S. A. (1981). The symbiotic marriage: A diagnostic profile. *Bulletin of the Menninger Clinic, 45*(2), 88-114.

Shereshefsky, P. M., & Yarrow, L. J. (1973). *Psychological aspects of a first pregnancy and early postnatal adaptation.* New York: Raven Press.

Shipley, W. C. (1940). A self-administering scale for measuring intellectual impairment and deterioration. *Journal of Psychology, 9*, 371-377.

Simmel, G. (1902). The number of members as determining the sociological form of the group. II. *American Journal of Sociology, 8*, 158-196.

Spainer, G. B., Sauer, W., & Larzelere, R. (1979). An empirical evaluation of the family life cycle. *Journal of Marriage and the Family, 41*(1), 27-38.

Speilberger, C. D., Gorsuch, R. L., & Lushsens, R. (1970). *State-Trait Anxiety Inventory.* Palo Alto, CA: Consulting Psychologists Press.

Spence, D. P. (1982). *Narrative truth and historical truth: Meaning and interpretation in psychoanalysis.* New York: W. W. Norton & Company.

Stern, D. N. (1985). *The interpersonal world of the infant.* New York: Basic Books.

Surrey, J. L. (1985). Self-in-relation: A theory of women's development. *Work in Progress.* Wellesley, MA: Wellesley College Stone Center for Developmental Services and Studies.

Terkelsen, K. G. (1980). Toward a theory of the family life cycle. In E. A. Carter & M. McGoldrick (Eds.), *The family life cycle: A framework for family therapy.* New York: Gardner Press, 21-52.

Thomas, C. B., & Greenstreet, R. L. (1973). Psychobiological characteristics in youth as predictors of five disease states: Suicide, mental illness, hypertension, coronary heart disease, and tumor. *Johns Hopkins Medical Journal,* 16-43.

Tienari, P., Sorri, A., Lahti, I., Naarala, M., Wahlberg, K., Ronkko, T., Pohjola, J., & Moring, J. (1985). The Finnish adoptive family study of schizophrenia. *The Yale Journal of Biology and Medicine, 58*, 227-237.

Vaillant, G. E. (1974). Natural history of male psychological health: II. *Archives of General Psychiatry, 31*, 15-22.

Vaillant, G. E. (1977). *Adaptation to Life.* Boston: Little, Brown, & Co.

Vaillant, G. E., & Milofsky, E. (1980). Natural history of male psychological health: XI. Empirical evidence for Erikson's model of the life cycle. *American Journal of Psychiatry, 137*, 1348-1359.

Watzlawick, P. (1984). Components of ideological "Realities." In P. Watzlawick (Ed.), *The invented reality.* New York: W. W. Norton & Company, 206-247.

Weissman, M. M. (May, 1980). *The epidemiology of depression in women: Prevalence, morbidity, and treatment.* Symposium conducted at the meeting of the American Psychiatric Association, San Francisco, CA.

Wenner, N. K., Cohen, M. B., Weigert, E. V., Kvarnes, R. G., Ohaneson, E. M. & Fearing, J. M. (1969). Emotional problems in pregnancy. *Psychiatry, 32*(4), 389-410.

Wolf, E. S. (1980). On the developmental line of selfobject relations. In A. Goldberg (Ed.), *Advances in self-psychology.* New York: International Universities Press, 117-130.

Worthington, E. L., Jr. (1987). Treatment of families during life transitions: Matching treatment to family responses. *Family Process, 26*(2), 295-308.

Worthington, E. L., Jr., & Buston, B. G. (1986). The marriage relationship during the transition to parenthood: A review and a model. *Journal of Family Issues, 7*(4), 443-473.

Wynne, L. C. (1984). The epigenesis of relational systems: A model for understanding family development. *Family Process, 23*(3), 297-318.

Wynne, L. C., & Singer, M. T. (1963). Thought disorders and family relations of schizophrenics. *Archives of General Psychiatry, 9*, 191-198.

Index